THE
COMING
ECONOMIC
EARTHQUAKE

A NATIONAL BEST-SELLER

LARRY BURKETT

THE COMING ECONOMIC EARTHQUAKE

REVISED AND UPDATED FOR THE CLINTON AGENDA

MOODY PRESS

CHICAGO

Scripture quotations, unless noted otherwise, are taken from the *New American Standard Bible,* © 1960, 1962, 1963, 1968, 1971, 1972, 1973, 1975, and 1977 by The Lockman Foundation. Used by permission.

ISBN: 0-8024-1539-3

5 7 9 10 8 6 4

Printed in the United States of America

CONTENTS

INTRODUCTION

I completed work on *The Coming Economic Earthquake* in March of 1991. It was the first of many books on the critical status of the U.S. economy that have hit the book stores around the country since that time. These books, along with Ross Perot, helped to focus the election of 1992 around the economy and, because of it, President Bush lost his job.

In truth, George Bush didn't create the problems in our economy; he inherited them. His first error was not taking any aggressive action to control government spending and stop the flood of debt at the national level. Unfortunately, he listened to his financial advisors, who themselves believed that debt and deficits don't matter. They do matter, because they sap the strength from the productive private sector.

His second error was agreeing with the Democrats in 1990 to raise taxes in exchange for spending caps, in contradiction to his promise of "no new taxes." His "read my lips" statement came back to haunt him many times during the campaign.

In all probability, the recession that started in 1990 was the result of too much consumer debt during the eighties. However, Bill Clinton successfully focused national attention on Republican economic policies (including the Bush tax increase) as the probable cause.

Then, upon attaining the presidency, Bill Clinton promptly raised taxes again to feed a new round of social programs he wanted to implement. This action doesn't send a mixed message, as some suggested. It clearly says, "Say one thing and do another."

In 1988 I wrote that I believed whoever was elected that year would be a one-term president and the economy would be his downfall. The election of '88 can be likened to that of being chosen captain of the Titanic—a great honor, but with disastrous consequences.

In 1992 the American people decided they didn't like "Captain" Bush, so they elected "Captain" Clinton, who has been airlifted onto the Titanic and is now steaming full speed toward the mid-Atlantic ice pack.

With the current state of our economy and the ever-growing debt of our government, there is almost no way Bill Clinton can survive the wrath of the voters in 1996, unless a third political party again splits the votes. Even then it would be very difficult since any candidate needs a majority in the electoral college.

I don't envy our president. He inherited a mess, which he has succeeded in making considerably worse.

In this updated and expanded version of *The Coming Economic Earthquake* book I will examine the consequences of the Omnibus Budget Reconciliation Act of 1993 (the Clinton tax bill), the Health Security Act, and the effects of the North American Free Trade Agreement (NAFTA). You'll find this in Part II.

I wish the health care issue was settled already, one way or the other, so that its full impact could be calculated. But it's not, so the best I can do is guess what the final package may be, based on the best information available. Certainly some form of health care "reform" is going to be adopted. I will look at the package the Clintons are pushing and evaluate its assets and liabilities.

Since *The Coming Economic Earthquake* book was first re-leased in September of 1991, some 550,000 copies have been sold. As a result I have had the opportunity to address members of the Congress several times, as well as sit in on many policy-making discussions about our economy.

I am continually amazed at how so many intelligent people can be so confused over such a simple issue as debt. Most average income Americans understand the bottom line very well: You can't spend more than you make forever.

Unfortunately most government economists get bogged down in their analysis of the debt as a ratio of the Gross Domestic Prod-uct or debt as a percentage of net domestic disposable income. More often than not, the discussions evolve into a debate over whether or not a $5 or $6 trillion debt is sustainable.

These arguments, in my opinion, are irrelevant. The national debt (currently quoted at $4.3 trillion) is nothing more than an accumulation of our government's annual deficits. It is the annu-al deficits that will be the ruin of our economy. The interest owed on the national debt simply adds to the annual deficits.

President Eisenhower often equated the cost of a battleship or submarine to the number of hospitals that could be built or high-ways constructed. Today, just the interest on the national debt costs every American family the equivalent of one years college expenses for each child. Families who can't afford to send their kids to college should feel heartened that, at least, they help to pay their "fair share" of the debt.

We have proved that we can manage a $4-trillion-plus debt. After all, we're doing it right now. If it were not for the annual interest payments, along with the additional deficit spending each year, we probably could muddle along indefinitely.

It's like a family, in debt up to their ears, who makes just enough to keep their payments current. They can get by unless something unscheduled happens—like a baby, a car breaking down, an accident, or an illness. Then they start down the road to disaster. This country is so far down the road to disaster now that, in my opinion, there is very little that can be done to avert it.

Recently, while driving, I happened upon a radio talk show where the host was discussing the economy. A comment he made

facetiously is, in large part, correct. He said, "The whole economic crisis in our nation is a hoax. There is really no $4 trillion debt.
There is no annual deficit of $300 billion. There is no lack of jobs
in America. And there is no problem starting businesses. If there
were," he went on to say, "no one would be stupid enough to do
what we're doing."

The point is well taken. In fact our national leaders are doing
almost exactly the opposite of what is required to recover this
economy and avert a major crisis. At a time when we should be
encouraging new businesses and supporting those already in existence, we're passing new regulations that make it harder to start
new businesses and create jobs. When we should be rewarding
thrift and encouraging savings, we are punishing those who are
successful and discouraging them from investing.

On the issue of taxes, perhaps the following maxim says it better than anyone today could (or would).

> You cannot bring about prosperity by discouraging thrift. You
> cannot strengthen the weak by weakening the strong. You cannot
> help the poor by destroying the rich. You cannot help the wage earn-
> er by pulling down the wage payer. You cannot build character and
> courage by taking away man's initiative.[1]

As cruel as it may sound, from the long-term perspective of the
economy, it would be better to raise taxes on the poor than on
the wealthy. It is only the wealthy—the people who have surplus
money—who are able to invest in industries that create the jobs
and wages that make it possible for the poor to escape their
poverty.

The Communists and Socialists argued for nearly 100 years
that this was not true—until they tried their philosophy in real
life. The result is what we now see in Russia and Eastern Europe:
poverty at every level.

Socialism, under the title of communism, held absolute authority in the former Soviet Union for more than 70 years. It will
be many years, perhaps decades, before these Socialists learn to
survive on their own. Even now, many Russians clamor for the
"good old days" when the central planning committees of the
Communist party allocated four potatoes a week per person. As I

recall, the Jews reacted similarly upon leaving the "security" of Egypt under Moses.

Recently I was discussing the economy with a businessman from Sweden, where they have some of the most restrictive regulations and highest taxes in the world. His comment to me was, "I would rather start a business in Sweden today than in America because we have seen our mistakes and are moving away from Socialism to a more free-market-enterprise system. In America, you are just now implementing the policies that we are abandoning."

There are some innovative ideas for how to rescue our economy now circulating in Washington. I will share a few of these in this expanded edition. At least when you write to your congressional representatives you will be able to point out that alternatives, other than just allowing the economy to self-destruct, do exist. Will any of these plans be implemented? I sincerely doubt it, because in every case they require some sacrifices to be made.

As Congressman Phil Crane (R-IL) recently said, "I believe we will just ride this thing out until the economy crashes and burns; then we'll see what we can salvage from the ashes."

I pray that he is wrong—for the sake of my grandchildren.

When Moody Press asked me to update *The Coming Economic Earthquake* book, I was somewhat hesitant. My concern in updating a book is that many people who bought the earlier edition might think we were just trying to sell them another copy of the same information. To avert this, in Part I, I have eliminated some of the previous chapters, and in the remaining chapters, if statistical information has changed significantly, that data has been updated. This way those who have read the earlier edition will have the latest available information. All the chapters in Part II are new. Hopefully we have done this in the least confusing fashion possible.

Bear in mind when reading this or any other book on the economy, although statistical sources are used and quoted, all such data requires some interpretation. Therefore, a lot of what I present is *my* interpretation of how that data will affect our future economy.

A good example of this is the 1993 Omnibus Budget Reconciliation Act, otherwise known as the Clinton Tax Act. Although there is a huge tax increase contained in this bill, it also contains some potential budget reductions. It is my opinion that few, if any, of these reductions will ever take place. I say that based on previous failed attempts to control the deficits. Once a little time passes, there is less and less incentive to cut spending. That is particularly true if the spending cuts take place after the next presidential election.

Thanks for taking the time to read this book. I sincerely pray that enough people will take this looming financial disaster seriously and will demand that *real* changes be made. But I have to be honest and say that I don't really believe they will. We have gone too far, and too many Americans are hooked on government handouts.

I fear Phil Crane is right and we will allow our economy to crash and burn. Then we'll salvage what we can from the ashes.

NOTE

1. For a number of years these maxims have been attributed to Abraham Lincoln. The author of the maxims is the Rev. William John Henry Boetcker, an ordained minister from Erie, Pennsylvania, born in 1873, who became a lecturer and pamphleteer. Mr. Boetcker first printed these maxims in 1916 in a leaflet entitled "Lincoln on Private Property." Originally, one side of the leaflet contained some words by Lincoln; the other side had maxims by Mr. Boetcker. It was republished in 1917, 1938, and 1945 by the Inside Publishing Company, which Mr. Boetcker apparently controlled.

PART ONE

1

AN ECONOMIC UPDATE

Without a doubt, the most common questions I am asked about the economy are: How long before the economy collapses? and, What can I do to protect my assets?

The first question is more difficult than the second, which is impossible. No one can accurately predict any specific economic event any more than someone can accurately predict the exact time of an earthquake. A lot of people have attempted both, with varying degrees of success (or failure).

There are enough people predicting the coming economic collapse . . . depression . . . inflation . . . whatever, that eventually one of them is bound to be right. It's like gamblers who bet on every horse; they are bound to win. Of course they spend more than they make, but their success rate is 100 percent.

Most of the economic "forecasting gurus" I've read about usually gained their fame by predicting correctly some major economic event. However, if you examine their track records before and after those individual events, they usually look pretty abysmal.

There are some exceptions. There always are but, in general, most good economists steer away from economic predictions—at least in terms of dates and times. Since I am neither an economist nor a prophet, I will stay well clear of specific predictions. However, there are some common points upon which we all can agree—with a high percentage of accuracy.

I am not a seismologist, but I can tell you that there have been major earthquakes in the southern California area, some along what is now called the San Andreas Fault. How do I know that? Because there is a *big* crack in the ground that can be seen as you fly over the area. I also can tell you that there will be *another* big earthquake in the same area—sometime. So it's not if, but *when,* that matters.

Seismology is still such an inexact science that seismologists can measure only the effects of earthquakes, not the causes. Until scientists know a lot more about *how* and *why* earthquakes occur in certain locations, they will not be able to predict accurately *when* they might occur. At present, seismologists wait until there are visible signs, such as ground movement, steam venting, or volcanic eruptions, before the local inhabitants are warned. Often, it is too late by then.

> *The low interest rates are a sign of a stagnant economy, and the low inflation rate simply reflects the inability of most businesses to pass along increased costs.*

Even when there were adequate warnings, as in the case of the eruption of Mount Saint Helens in Washington state, many people refused to believe them because of past false alarms. Those who lived near the dormant volcano had heard it rumble from time to time, always to recede into submission. They presumed incorrectly that, since the mountain had been peaceful since they were born, it would remain so forever.

The same basic logic can be applied to the coming economic earthquake—at least in part. When you see steam and ashes venting from a long dormant volcano, common sense should tell you that something is about to happen. When you see steam and ashes venting from cracks in our economy, that should be considered a portent of things to come also.

Many noted economists don't believe that our economy will collapse. In spite of mounting statistical evidence that a major eruption is brewing, they insist that at the last possible moment something will happen to solve our problems. Some think it will come in the form of a technological revolution that will create whole new industries to replace those we have lost.

Others think it will be a sudden wave of fiscal responsibility that will sweep over our government; and our politicians will vote to cut spending, cut taxes, cut regulations, and make the free enterprise system function again.

Still others simply believe the problems aren't as bad as they have been made out to be. They interpret the recent low inflation and low interest rates as evidence that things are turning around.

What they don't see, in my opinion, is an economy being hamstrung by excessive government regulations, an aging work force expecting to retire on government largess, and a national attitude that our government can make better economic decisions than private industry can. The low interest rates are a sign of a stagnant economy, and the low inflation rate simply reflects the inability of most businesses to pass along increased costs.

If you could sit and talk with a housewife, an average worker, and someone in business, all of whom lived through the Great Depression, they would definitely provide an education on wishful thinking.

The housewife would remember how positive the news was just prior to the stock market crash of '29. The country was experiencing an all-time high in economic output, and jobs were plentiful. Living standards were rising rapidly, and immigrants were pouring into America, the land of opportunity.

The average worker would relate how positive things were in industry during the late twenties. There were plenty of jobs in the rapidly expanding industrial sector, even for those with virtually no education. Farm hands were leaving the rural environment, where work weeks of 100 hours or more were common, to seek jobs in the automotive factories of Detroit, which paid twice the wages they had earned for half the hours they had worked. Certainly, by our standards today their living conditions were meager, but compared to those of just 10 years earlier they were luxuriant.

The businessperson would tell you that there were alarmists even in the mid-twenties who tried to spread a message of gloom and doom over the rapid expansion of the stock market and the practice of leverage (credit) to buy equities in American companies. But these voices were muted by the assurances that, with the Federal Reserve in place and the massive expansion in consumer goods, there was no problem. Sure, stock prices were high, but Americans were assured by their stockbrokers that the economy had not come close to reaching its peak.

Politicians of the pre-depression era confidently asserted that Americans were living in an era of unprecedented prosperity that would continue for decades. Then, along came the stock market crash of '29, followed by a wave of protectionism as politicians tried to slam the door on the foreign producers who were invading their constituents' territory.

The net result was that the recession of 1929 turned into the depression of 1932. The American voters, unaccustomed to hard times, elected a new president, Franklin Roosevelt, who promised to solve the economic problems through government intervention (sound familiar?).

Ultimately World War II ended the Great Depression but not Roosevelt's social programs. America came dangerously close to a dictatorship during the Roosevelt administration—so much so that Congress passed a constitutional amendment limiting future presidents to two consecutive terms in office.

Two generations have come and gone since the lessons of the Great Depression were learned. Let us not forget that we just think we're smarter than they were.

HOW LONG DO WE HAVE AND HOW BAD WILL IT GET?

After reviewing the economic data for *The Coming Economic Earthquake* book in 1990–91, I came to the conclusion that the ever-increasing deficits would exhaust all sources of government income sometime around the year 2000. I also assumed that our government would not do anything blatantly foolish, such as raise taxes or further increase federal regulation of businesses.

In reality, taxes have been raised—not just once (1990 Omnibus Budget Reconciliation Act under Bush), but twice (1993 Omnibus Budget Reconciliation Act). The first tax increase was in the range of $30 billion a year. The second was in the range of $50 billion per year. Each promised a reduction in government spending to justify the tax increases. Neither has materialized to date. That is, the promised spending cuts have not materialized. The tax increases definitely have materialized.

It is not possible to remove the better part of $80 billion a year in spendable income from the private sector of our economy without having an effect. When money is diverted from private hands and given to the government, it simply means there is less spending in the private sector. This eventually results in a slower economy, less industry, and lower employment.

Obviously some portion of the money that is diverted to the government works its way back into the private sector economy, but it is watered down by the typical government inefficiencies. Most government income (taxes) is taken from those with a surplus who would otherwise invest it in the economy.

Welfare at every level, from the inner city poor to the elderly, is destroying the morale as well as the economic base of our nation.

Even the most socialized economist in the world would admit that people's spending patterns change as their economic status changes. Once basic needs, such as food, shelter, and transportation are met, people look for the best places to invest.

It is that need to maximize return that fuels any nation's economic growth. It doesn't matter whether you are for or against social programs. The fact is, more money in the hands of bureaucrats to give away means less money in the pockets of citizens to spend or invest.

Allow me to illustrate. Let's assume that a tax increase, such as the 1993 law, takes money from the private sector and "redistributes" it through the government. In the case of the '93 bill, about one-half of the proposed increase in taxes was to come from upper-income people. The rest was to come from across-the-board increases through gas taxes and such.

Regardless of the rhetoric, such tax increases are nothing more than welfare economics: taking from the haves to give to the have-nots. Most Christians would agree that it's important to care for the poor. From a biblical perspective, that's absolutely true, but the involuntary transfer of wealth from one group of taxpayers to another is *not* charity. It is socialism.

Welfare never helps the poor. It merely traps them at the lowest level. Welfare at every level, from the inner city poor to the elderly, is destroying the morale as well as the economic base of our nation. The statistical evidence of this abounds.

You could write an entire book on the evils of government-sponsored welfare and the certain economic collapse of our nation if we don't bring it under control; but others already have done so. One excellent book on this topic is *Losing Ground* by Charles Murray. Everyone should read it—especially black Americans.

Welfare has done to recipient black families what 150 years of slavery could not do: It has destroyed their moral foundation. The strong underpinning of the black family in America has always been its deep spiritual roots. Embedded within the spiritual principles of God's Word is a strong work ethic, as well as a strong commitment to family values.

Welfare has destroyed the work ethic, as well as the core family of those who have learned to live on it—from the strong black family in the 1950s, when less than 2 percent of black children were born to unwed mothers, to 1993, when the percentage is approximately 68 percent.

In some areas, such as Harlem and South Central Los Angeles, the illegitimacy rate is closer to 80 percent. Aid to Families with Dependent Children (AFDC) and other welfare programs have encouraged pregnant teens to move out on their own, have multiple children, and never get married.

This problem is not isolated to the black community by any means. It simply has progressed more rapidly in this targeted community. Among whites the illegitimacy rate has increased from about 3 percent in 1963 to nearly 22 percent in 1993.[1]

The fundamental difference in the white community is that children are often put up for adoption or are cared for by other family members, much as they were in the black community prior to welfare. However, I have no doubt that if this trend of government-supported welfare, along with the permissive attitudes of our society, continues at the same rate, we will have the same problems in every community in America.

Perhaps the greatest advantage that non-black families have is that our economy will run out of money before the total destruction of all family values can be accomplished. Even now several states are acting to reform their welfare programs.

The point I reemphasize here is that once money is taken out of the productive sector and redistributed into the non-productive sector (and with rare exception I include all government spending in this category), everyone suffers—especially the poor.

Even if all discretionary spending were cut by 25 percent ($135 billion), the government still would not come close to balancing its budget.

Too often they don't even realize it, but the jobs they need to get a start in life don't exist. A dollar in taxes paid by a business or individual is not really just a dollar of disposable income lost. The average business operates on a 4 to 6 percent of gross-income-profit margin.

Therefore, each additional dollar confiscated by the government took about $16 of sales to generate. A mere one percent increase in taxes reduces a business' investment capital by 16 percent! To make that up, the business must generate 16 percent more sales—tough to do in a slow economy.

To realize just how devastating this transfer-of-wealth mentality is to our future economic health, you only need to view the facts. Remember, all government spending comes at the cost of economic growth. In 1962 all entitlements took $32 billion (28 percent of all government spending). In 1995 they will consume $795 billion (50.4 percent of all government spending).

In 1962 interest payments on the national debt consumed $6.9 billion of taxpayers' dollars (6.1 percent of all government spending). In 1995 interest will take $244 billion (15.5 percent of all government spending).

Growth of Entitlement Spending

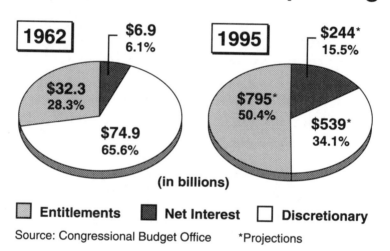

(in billions)

☐ Entitlements   ■ Net Interest   ☐ Discretionary

Source: Congressional Budget Office   *Projections

Discretionary (non-entitlement) spending was $74.9 billion in 1962 (65.6 percent of all government spending). In 1995 it will be $539 billion (only 34.1 percent of all government spending).

As a percentage of government spending, entitlements and interest have nearly doubled and discretionary spending has declined by nearly 50 percent. Even if all discretionary spending were cut by 25 percent ($135 billion), the government still would not come close to balancing its budget.

Economic *growth,* along with spending controls, is the most viable solution to our looming economic crisis (at least the *politi-*

cally possible solution). The difficulty is that we are doing the exact opposite. Entitlements continue to grow, while our political leaders continue to do everything possible to choke off economic growth.

EXPAND GOVERNMENT = SHRINK BUSINESS

Under Republican leadership, the probability of avoiding an economic calamity (caused by massive government deficits) was slim. Perhaps the only real chance we had was to deregulate the economy, cut personal income taxes, cut government spending, and recreate a free market economy. Then perhaps the economy could have recovered sufficiently to close the deficit gap and pay down some of the debt.

At a time when common sense should be dictating lower tax rates, the Clinton administration is steadily increasing the money drain on American families.

To do this would have been painful, and nearly every recipient of government largess would have had to accept cuts in the automatic cost-of-living increases built into Social Security, Medicare, federal retirement, and such.

Clearly, that is not going to happen now. I don't mean to imply that somehow George Bush was a super conservative with a commitment to controlling government growth. Clearly his four-year record reflects a bias toward bigger government and more regulation of private business.

But compared to Bill Clinton, George Bush was a staunch conservative—in the mold of Teddy Roosevelt. What George Bush failed to do was follow through on Ronald Reagan's economic policy. Bill Clinton is dismantling the free enterprise system and expanding every phase of government control.

At a time when common sense should be dictating lower tax rates, the Clinton administration is steadily increasing the money drain on American families. In an economy that is not creating enough new jobs for those entering the work force, much less those who are being laid off, the government should be reducing the regulatory burdens on businesses. Instead, it is expanding them to new horizons.

If you want a good analysis of what government regulations are costing every American family, I would suggest reading *What Ever Happened to the American Dream* (Moody Press). Our economy could expand by 30 to 50 percent, and our budget could be balanced in 5 years—just through deregulations and government downsizing.

A classic example of government regulation out of control can be seen in a recent story from California. In a state staggering under massive defense cutbacks, falling land values, and escalating unemployment, a fly (yes, a *fly*) has been added to the endangered species list. The Delhi Sands fly threatens to shut down one of California's major farming areas.

The penalty for killing one of these flies is a fine of up to $200,000, and a jail term of one year.[2] So much for common sense in America, huh?

The cost of government regulations is both direct and indirect.

DIRECT COSTS

The direct cost can be seen in regulations such as the Clean Water Act: Developers must pay for extensive land evaluations before they can develop a piece of property, and they also must comply with a myriad of state and local ordinances, each of which add additional overhead and, ultimately, cost to the buyer.

Some regulations are reasonable and are meant to protect other citizens from exposure to hazardous wastes or polluted drinking water. But, without question, as the regulations have increased and the regulatory agencies have expanded, they are killing whole industries. The cost of regulation is a tax on every American—pure and simple.

The greatest risk to freedom, as well as cost in regulatory controls, comes from the federal government. Federal regulations are created in Washington but are expected to be applied uniformly throughout the entire country. Common sense should tell us that is illogical. There is simply no way that EPA standards, designed for worst case situations like Los Angeles and New York City, should be applied in places like Sylacauga, Alabama or Erie, Pennsylvania. And yet, they are.

In addition, many of these federal regulations are based on faulty scientific data (at best). In the opinions of many noted scientists, many of whom are neither politically conservative nor Christian, the billions we are spending to solve global warming, heal the ozone, and eliminate pesticides are based on "voodoo" science.

More and more scientists are stepping up to confront the radicals with the truth: The only real hole in the ozone is in the ozone depletion theory advanced by the radical environmentalists in Washington. The only global warming is in the homes and cars of people who will no longer have freon to cool their cars and houses. And the only real danger with most of our pesticides is that the environmental radicals think there are too many people in the world and hope that the elimination of pesticides will thin them out.

Excessive and abusive government regulations represent the greatest threat to American industry and the creation of new jobs.

Dr. Bruce N. Ames, whose pollution monitoring system is the standard in most scientific circles, recently commented on the proposed ban on commercial pesticides by the EPA. I didn't record his exact words, but the gist was: There are more carcinogens in one cup of coffee than in all the foods you eat in an entire year.

When asked what he thought about the ban on pesticides by the EPA, Dr. Ames commented, "Americans won't like finding worms in their corn or weevils in their bread. And they won't like the price they will pay for the food they need."

I could fill a whole book with horror stories about businesses and individuals who have been destroyed emotionally and financially by government agencies such as the EPA, OSHA, EEOC, and others. The majority of these alleged violations occurred before the regulations even existed.

The Constitution explicitly prohibits *ex post facto* law: passing laws that are retroactive. This rule means that government cannot pass a law today that makes an act done 10 or 20 years ago illegal; and yet, our regulatory agencies do so today with impunity.

The classic example of this has to be the case against the manufacturers of asbestos. Thousands of companies have been sued for violations of current laws that were not in effect at the time of offense. This is truly *ex post facto* law. Under this same rule of law, an obstetrician could be sued 20 years after delivering a baby for failure to use a medical procedure that did not exist at the time of the baby's birth.

If you think this can't happen, you need to read some of the current court decisions. The fact is, it's happening now; companies are being sued under current environmental laws that didn't exist when the alleged offenses occurred. Understandably *ex post facto* laws make many companies wary of operating within the United States. So they move to developing countries that offer them protection from retroactive liability.

I can guarantee you that anyone who has experienced the trauma of an EPA Superfund confrontation never will do business again with any chemical or recycling company.

In many instances the major factor in a company relocating to another country is not labor costs. American labor may cost more per hour than that of other countries, but their per-product cost is often lower. It is the threat of lawsuits and excessive regulations that drive most businesses out.

I have discussed the so-called Superfund Site Law in other books, but it is the classic example of government regulation running amok in private industry. Never has this been a more blatant example of the rights of private individuals, especially business owners, being ignored.

At a recent conference a couple came up to ask if I knew anyone who could help them. They had just received a notice from the EPA that they were liable under the Superfund Law for a "share" of the cleanup costs for a lead reprocessing plant. The EPA informed them that their share would amount to nearly $300,000. The wife sobbed as she told me this would destroy them financially; their total worth was far less than that amount.

It seems the husband had the misfortune of making his living for a short while (between jobs) by collecting old batteries and selling them to recycling companies. Now one might think this was a worthy environmental effort since, otherwise, these batteries might have been dumped into ditches and backyards and, thus, would have polluted the environment. But in the madness of our regulatory mania, common sense seems to be a lost art.

Instead of congratulating this small scale entrepreneur, the government sued him as a polluter when one of the recycling companies he had sold batteries to filed for bankruptcy protection after the EPA declared their plant a Superfund site.

I can guarantee you that anyone who has experienced the trauma of an EPA Superfund confrontation never will do business again with any chemical or recycling company.

Put yourself in the position of a successful businessman, like a friend I have in a southern city. For 30 years he operated a successful chemical company, which he started from scratch. He provided an assortment of chemical cleaning agents to major corporations, which then used them to produce needed industrial cleaning supplies—all in compliance with the laws in existence.

My friend sold his company in the late seventies and settled down to what he thought would be a peaceful retirement. Unfortunately, several of the companies he sold chemicals to now have been declared Superfund sites, and he has been brought into the legal action by the EPA—personally. No one claims that he ever polluted or even contributed to pollution. His only "crime" was making a profit when the government needed money.

A good, EPA-knowledgeable attorney costs about $300 an hour, whether you win or lose. My friend probably is looking at a total legal bill of $600,000 to $800,000 minimum, with no assurance that he will win in court. Of course, the EPA's attorneys are funded with our tax dollars.

One of the most direct assaults on American free enterprise is the assault on the winners in our economic system. For most of the history of our nation, hard work, thrift, and success were admired and appreciated. After all, in the process of making his millions, Henry Ford created millions of jobs at higher wages than ever before in history.

Most of the well-to-do in our society didn't steal their money; nor did they inherit it; they earned it. According to researcher Dr. Thomas J. Stanley, only about 10 percent of the millionaires in America inherited their wealth. The study also showed that 46 percent of all millionaires obtained their wealth through a business they started. Another 29 percent made it through a professional practice. And 33 percent accumulated wealth through corporate employment. So the vast majority of wealthy people *made* their money—many in spite of growing up in poverty themselves.[3]

In an effort to strike a chord with the populace, the Clinton administration hit upon the theme of making the rich pay their "fair share." In spite of all the evidence that, as a group, the upper 10 percent of all wage earners now pay twice as much as they did 20 years ago, the public bought this sales pitch. So we taxed the rich. I think we need to remember the old saying: You cannot strengthen the weak by weakening the strong.

When the attitude of the average American is to punish those who are successful, the economy is in real trouble. Unless the average American aspires to success, for others as well as themselves, we will develop the mind-set the Socialists want: equality —everyone poor.

After watching the Clinton administration's performance for the last year, I have concluded that the majority of economic changes have been for the worse rather than the better. As I have said before, the only real options available to any president since Ronald Reagan are either to accelerate or decelerate the downhill slide. Apparently, President Clinton has opted to hurry up and get it over with.

Although the short-term annual deficits are somewhat lower than originally projected, with the government now financing much of its debt in the short-term bond market to take advantage of the lower rates, the slightest upward tick in interest rates will send the annual deficits spiraling out of control. In addition, the so-called entitlement programs, which now consume nearly 70 percent of all spending, are beyond the reach of anyone in Washington, including the president.

It should be clear to the most casual observer that the current administration has no grasp of common-sense economics. That is not surprising since the president and most of his advisors have grown up in a liberal political environment, and many have never actually worked in the free enterprise system.

I'm sure the president actually *believes* that bigger government is the solution to every social ill and that politicians, especially the new liberals, are able to allocate the nation's resources better than private individuals are.

Unfortunately for America, the Clinton administration is leading us down the same economic road that Europe and Russia have already gone. Those countries are trying desperately to abandon centralized planning and reduce entitlements, even while we continue to nationalize our economy.

The damage that can be done to our economy, as they expand social programs and government regulations, will bring this economy to a grinding halt.

The economics of the Clinton administration are not much different than those of the New Deal under Franklin Roosevelt or the Great Society under Lyndon Johnson. The only difference is that we no longer have the surplus capacity to feed these social experiments.

Ronald Reagan had one chance to salvage our economy when he first took office. His mandate from the voters was a *true* mandate. Nearly 80 percent of all voters cast their ballots for him. After cutting tax rates in 1981, he agreed to a "tax increases now and spending cuts later" package in 1982. With that agreement, he lost the last real opportunity to rein in government spending.

Within a year, the Congress once again had control over the nation's purse strings and continued the upward spiral of deficit spending. Although actual tax revenues to the federal government increased from approximately $600 billion to $1 trillion during the Reagan years (in contrast to what candidate Clinton said), actual spending increased from $678 billion to $1.1 trillion. Thus, the national debt was increased by nearly $2 trillion under President Reagan.

President Bush never had the mandate awarded Reagan and, in fact, rode in on the popularity of his predecessor. Bill Clinton slipped into the White House with a minority vote (43 percent) because of the voter split caused by Ross Perot's third party. Neither President Bush nor President Clinton had the confidence of the voters.

It is not the policies of President Clinton that are destroying our economy. He is a consummate politician who will compromise to either side to stay in office. But he is indebted to a group of radicals who have a clear agenda and total dedication to it: absolute governmental control! They will spend this economy into poverty to socialize America.

The damage that can be done to our economy, as they expand social programs and government regulations, will bring this economy to a grinding halt.

But remember, the Clinton administration is not the problem. It's a symptom! The real problem is a lack of moral and spiritual values at all levels of our society; otherwise, this administration never could have reached the White House.

NOTES

1. Thomas McArdle, "Moral Crisis of the Underclass," *Investor's Business Daily,* 11/10/93; Charles Murray, "The Coming White Underclass, *The Wall Street Journal,* 10/29/93.

2. Larry Gerber, "Protected Status for California Fly Has Local Officials Worried About Jobs," *Orlando Sentinel,* 10/12/93.

3. Thomas J. Stanley, "Why You're Not As Wealthy As You Should Be," *Medical Economics,* 7/20/92.

2

THE GREAT DEPRESSION

The following is a narrated description of the events that took place the week of October 24-30, 1929. The narration is my creation; the events are historical fact.

Due to one of those quirks of fate, the president of the New York Stock Exchange, Edward Simmons, was in Hawaii on his honeymoon the last week of October 1929. His vice president, Richard Whitney, was in charge. Whitney had a long history as a habitual gambler and was deeply indebted to the New York banking interests. He was appointed as the president of the New York Stock Exchange in 1930, but later he went to prison for "insider trading."

Richard Whitney sat looking out the window of his twelfth-story office, trying to focus his mind on the current crisis but, no matter how hard he tried, he could not make any sense out of what was happening.

Can Bernard Baruch be right? he thought. *No, it's impossible. There is simply no way the market can collapse. We're the strongest economy in the world. We sell our products to every other nation on Earth. Just the label "Made in America" stands for quality. Sure, the market has taken a hit, but the companies are still sound.*

He recalled the previous week when the whole of Wall Street had gone crazy. October 24 was a nightmare. As the buying frenzy hit the trading floor, Whitney saw something he would never forget as long as he lived, and he prayed to God he would never see again: nearly twelve million shares of common stocks traded in a single afternoon. No sooner had one level of trading been established than another ten thousand shares were offered. The men who had manipulated the sell-off were like sharks waiting for their victims to bleed to death. They refused to buy until the prices dropped to their predetermined level. Even AT&T, GE, and GM plummeted to dangerous lows as panic-stricken investors, fearing a market collapse, sold off shares.

Although few men realized it at the time, the finances of America were in shambles, and the thin veneer of prosperity covered a festering wound.

Whitney would have closed the exchange, but he feared the resulting reaction would be even worse. Besides, he knew President Hoover would be very irritated if he intervened in the market. The president believed in a free market, where the buyers and sellers established the rules.

But I know the bankers are manipulating this market for their own benefit, Whitney thought grimly. *They make more on their stock portfolios than they do on loans these days. They pump up a stock and then dump it on the unsuspecting little guys. The newspapers grovel at their feet and hype their stocks so that the whole country is in the market now.*

It's like Baruch said at lunch last week: "When the shoeshine boy starts giving tips on hot stocks to buy, it's time to get out of the market."

I really fear what could happen if we don't get some control over these swings in prices, Whitney thought as he went back over the day's trading. *We've lost almost $100 million in equity in the last week. Well, tomorrow is Friday. If we can weather this storm, maybe common sense will prevail by Monday*, he told himself without any real conviction.

What Whitney didn't know was that since the big traders had sold out at top price on the 24th, they intended to drive the prices down even further by calling the loans of some of the margin traders who were stretched thin. If the bankers could force them to sell in the down market, prices would plummet. Then they would re-buy their original stocks and pocket the difference.

"A smart man makes his money with money," J. P. Morgan was often heard to say, and, "God wouldn't have made sheep if he didn't expect them to be sheared."

Although few men realized it at the time, the finances of America were in shambles, and the thin veneer of prosperity covered a festering wound. The industrialists and bankers had succeeded in getting laws passed by the federal government that profited them greatly while undermining the economy as a whole.

The country was on a roll, and no one really thought it would come to an end.

America was producing more than the country could consume internally. Through the use of high-interest loans, borrowers were transferring their wealth to the industrialists and bankers on a scale never witnessed before. The industrialists, with their political power, had been instrumental in getting Congress to pass restrictive trade laws limiting imports. As they lost more of their foreign markets due to retaliatory restrictions, inventories were backing up. Unemployment was becoming a chronic problem for the "underclass." Production was slowing down. And loans were becoming commonplace.

The bankers were making huge "paper" profits through loans that often carried interest rates of 20 percent or more. The competition for loans became so intense that bankers eased loan qualifications to attract more borrowers.

The average American watched the money merchants getting wealthy in the stock market and flocked to the market to "strike it rich." Lacking the capital to invest, they financed a large portion of their speculation with the bankers. With virtually no controls on market trading, any speculator could hold blocks of stocks with as little as 10 percent down. If that stock was then used as collateral for more loans, the ratio could easily be fifty-to-one.

It was a win-win situation for the lenders. They loaned the money for small investors to buy the very stocks they themselves were forcing up through manipulation. Then, when the prices fell, the small speculators would borrow more to cover their losses. It was one of the most massive transfers of wealth in the history of civilization. It was the era of "paper" prosperity—the Roaring Twenties, when America could do no wrong. The country was on a roll, and no one really thought it would come to an end.

There were those voices of "doom and gloom" who shook their fingers and clicked their tongues, but their ominous predictions of calamity had not come true—yet.

On Monday, October 28, the New York Stock Exchange opened normally. Richard Whitney arrived at his Wall Street office at 7:00 A.M., as was his custom. Inwardly he was full of apprehension, though he tried his best not to show it. He had spent the weekend calling in every favor he had accumulated over the past ten years. His greatest fear was a run on the market by nervous investors who had the entire weekend to discuss the previous week's losses with their barroom buddies. He knew many, if not most, were heavily leveraged and could scarcely afford any further losses.

Sunday evening he had called Charles Mitchell of the National City Bank. "Charles, I need your help," he said as he unconsciously fingered the phone wire.

"What is it, Richard?" the banker asked, showing his irritation at being interrupted on the weekend. The all-day session on Saturday with his directors had been fatiguing enough. The bank's questionable debt list was growing at an alarming rate. *That's justice*, he thought. *They pressure me to make loans, then wonder why we have a collection problem.*

"I'm concerned that we may have a run tomorrow," Whitney said. "I want your guarantee that you and the others will support the market if necessary."

"Richard, there's not going to be any run on the market. Not tomorrow. Not ever. The country is doing just fine, and the market hasn't nearly reached its peak. We just pulled a little capital out. It will recover this week."

"I hope you're right." Whitney replied, with concern evident in his voice. "But I still want your word that you'll support the market if necessary. I don't want you pulling the plug on credit and sinking the whole ship."

"I guarantee that we'll support you, Richard. But I'm telling you, you're worrying too much. The country is sound, business is good, and we've got a president who understands how to keep the government off our backs. Now take it easy."

The traders were all assembled in the trading room of the exchange by eight o'clock that Monday morning. Each had a preset agenda for the trading he would do that day. Each would also try to hide his agenda until the others made a move. Promptly at nine o'clock the bell rang, and trading got underway. Richard Whitney watched from his glassed-in office to see what direction the market would follow. He almost called Mitchell again, but decided against it. *No sense in panicking*, he told himself.

The pace on the floor was frenzied as buyers and sellers jockeyed for position. The buyers were looking for bargains. The sellers were waiting in hopes that demand would drive the prices up. Shares began trading rapidly as cash-strapped smaller investors offered to sell some of their stocks.

By ten o'clock there was no definitive trend; the buyers and sellers were about even, with only a slight downward drift.

Whitney slumped back in his leather chair in relief. "That's fine," he said to the board auditor. "We can handle a drift downward. *We dodged the bullet this time*, he said mentally.

By the close of trading at four o'clock, the averages had dropped by twenty points. *Not an abnormal trading loss for the market on any given down day*, Whitney thought as he stuffed the latest trading reports into his briefcase and headed out the door. Normally he would have reviewed the reports before leaving, but he was mentally exhausted. The tension had kept him uptight for nearly a week now, and somehow he sensed it wasn't entirely over yet.

Millions of Americans lost their life savings, and thousands of millionaires became more statistics in the growing ranks of the unemployed.

On Tuesday, October 29, the market opened just as it had for two decades. No one had any particular sense of apprehension or anxiety. Most of the major traders assumed that Monday had been the real test of the market's resiliency; and although it had not set any growth records, at least there were no major cracks either.

When the Exchange opened for business, the trading volume quickly reached the level of the previous day, except that virtually all the trades were sell orders. The market plunged as more sellers flooded the floor. Once the plunge started, it was like Whitney's worst nightmare. The radio carried the bad news to the American people and more sell orders flooded in from panic-stricken investors, fearful of losing their savings. It was like a gigantic economic snowball—as more sellers panicked, fewer buyers would step forward.

As the frenzied trading continued, even the veteran traders knew this was not just another down day on the market. It was a true sell-off of all stocks. Even the traditional "blue chippers" were being dumped.

By the ending bell, AT&T was down 100 points, General Motors down 150 points, General Electric down 90 points. More than 16 million shares were traded at a loss of $10 billion—twice the amount of currency in the entire country at that time. Whitney knew that without major support from the big banks, the market would continue the tumble when the bell sounded the next morning. Even with their support, he wasn't at all sure the selling could be halted.

The evening newspapers all carried the headline: "Wall Street Crashes." By the next morning, virtually every small investor in the country had issued a sell order, hoping to salvage something of their equity.

Panic ruled the market from that fateful Tuesday on. There were small rallies where determined investors attempted to support their portfolio of stocks. But those who did quickly found themselves among the destitute. Millions of Americans lost their life savings, and thousands of millionaires became just more statistics in the growing ranks of the unemployed.

People who had grown up in the American enterprise system and thought it could not be defeated were swallowed up as banks, businesses, farms, and homes all fell victim to what would be called "The Great Depression."

One story in a New York newspaper told of a ship full of wealthy entrepreneurs who, on the return portion of their vacations, sailed from England the last week of October. The ship had been equipped with the latest telegraph equipment so the men could keep abreast of their stocks during the voyage. By the 30th of October, as the market plummeted, they could no longer place sell orders and expect them to be executed, and by the time they arrived in New York on the 4th of November, they owned little more than what they had with them on the ship.

One of the most publicized aspects of the Wall Street collapse was the specter of suicides by once-prominent traders. Men who had lost their entire fortunes often committed suicide by jumping from their offices high above Wall Street. But as alarming as this was, it paled when compared to the misery the average American worker and his family suffered over the succeeding decade.

By the end of the year, the Stock Market had lost the unbelievable sum of $40 billion in equity, taking with it hundreds of banks and millions of jobs. By 1932, the depth of the Depression, more than five thousand banks had closed their doors; leaving millions of depositors with nothing to show for their thrift. The national income plummeted from over $80 billion in 1929 to less than $40 billion by 1932. The promise of prosperity built on debt had tempted normally conservative Americans to risk all they owned. They lost.

In 1928 there was no venture too harebrained for a banker to fund, if the interest rate was high enough. By 1930 there was no legitimate venture, no matter what its merit, that could find an interested banker. Speculators, such as Bernard Baruch, who had withdrawn their assets from the market before the collapse, used their hard currency to buy land, businesses, and the lifetime efforts of others for a fraction of their actual worth. Even the "big banks" were on the ropes. The men who had manipulated the market for their own benefit found the pond rapidly drying up.

What we accept as normal today, any generation prior to the Great Depression would have seen as unconstitutional.

Hypocritically, most of those who had once insisted that the government should stay out of the regulating business now cried for government aid. Their cries fell on deaf ears in the White House. Herbert Hoover had been elected because of his *laissez-faire* policy, and he was not about to renege on what he believed. He did attempt a few government programs to help the unemployed and homeless, but most were aimed at easing poverty, not stimulating business. His philosophy was, "If business created the mess, business should repair it."

Most economists since the Depression have faulted Hoover for his nonintervention. Perhaps a good case can be made for the administration's lack of control prior to the Depression, but there had been several previous depressions in America from which the nation recovered without direct government intervention, so the president felt justified in following historical precedent.

Without a government bailout, using taxpayers' money, the Depression of 1837 had lasted but four years; the Depression of

1893, four years; and the panics (recessions) of 1904, 1907, and 1921 lasted less than two years each.

But with millions of voters out of work, and the big banks in trouble, Hoover could garner no support for his reelection. The nation was ready for a change: a "New Deal," as the Democratic party promised.

Their spokesman for this New Deal was an articulate aristocrat with a household family name: Roosevelt. Franklin Roosevelt was born to wealth, raised in wealth, and educated in wealth at Harvard.

Later, Roosevelt was exposed to the economic philosophies of Dr. John Maynard Keynes of England. In essence, Keynes believed increased government spending and heavy regulation of banking and business could avoid depressions and ensure prosperity. This philosophy was not entirely new. Karl Marx had advocated some of the same ideas.

The Depression set the stage for the federal government to dominate American business, banking, commerce, and the economy as a whole.

Keynes' economic theory had yet to be tested in a sizeable system. But, with America in depression, it was about to be implemented wholeheartedly. That now suited the bankers and industrialists perfectly because they desperately needed an infusion of capital to hold on to what they had siphoned out of the general public. The New Deal would forevermore change the average American's view of the role of their central government.

I have presented this brief overview of the Depression of 1929 because so few Americans are aware of how it began—or ended. Most of those who lived through the Depression were scarred for life. Most unemployed voters viewed Franklin Roosevelt as truly their economic "savior." And in fairness, President Roosevelt did what he believed was the right thing to do, in spite of the Supreme Court's view to the contrary. But so profoundly is the New Deal philosophy now ingrained in American politics that, in order to understand the coming "economic earthquake," it is critical to understand how our government functions monetarily.

What we accept as normal today, any generation prior to the Great Depression would have seen as unconstitutional. According to the Constitution, the central (federal) government is to have no powers except those specifically granted it by the Constitution. All other rights and powers not specifically granted the individual states are preserved for their citizens. That includes the right to succeed or fail according to one's own abilities, unrestrained by the government. So fearful were the founders of this country of a strong central government that they went to great lengths to ensure that its powers were severely limited. Basically, the central government could settle arguments between the states, organize an army to defend the nation's common cause, regulate interstate commerce, and negotiate foreign treaties. The federal government was allowed to raise its operating capital by charging an interstate tariff on goods only—period!

The Depression set the stage for the federal government to dominate American business, banking, commerce, and the economy as a whole. Franklin Roosevelt raised the status of the federal government to that of the "great provider." Whether or not you agree or disagree with the New Deal, no one can deny it changed American politics and the economy forever.

In my opinion, it also set the stage for an eventual economic disaster unparalleled in American history. As you will see, the events that led us to this point are not unique. Others have traveled this economic road before us. The major difference between us and them is our size and influence. It is my considered opinion that our nation has prospered because of a unique commitment to God's divine authority. We are now traveling a path that is almost totally contrary to that original commitment. It would be wise to note God's instruction to the Jews:

Now it shall be, if you will diligently obey the Lord your God, being careful to do all His commandments which I command you today, the Lord your God will set you high above all the nations of the earth. And all these blessings shall come upon you and overtake you, if you will obey the Lord your God. Blessed shall you be in the city, and blessed shall you be in the country. . . . The Lord will open for you His good storehouse, the heavens, to give rain to your land in its season and to bless all the work of your hand; and you shall lend to many nations, but you shall not borrow. And the Lord shall make you the head and not the tail, and you only shall be above, and you shall not be underneath, if you will listen to the commandments of the Lord your God, which I charge you today, to observe them carefully, and do not turn aside from any of the words which I command you today, to the right or to the left, to go after other gods to serve them (Deuteronomy 28:1-3, 12-14).

Now observe His warning to them:

But it shall come about, if you will not obey the Lord your God, to observe to do all His commandments and His statutes with which I charge you today, that all these curses shall come upon you and overtake you. . . . The alien who is among you shall rise above you higher and higher, but you shall go down lower and lower. He shall lend to you but you shall not lend to him; he shall be the head, and you shall be the tail. So all these curses shall come on you and pursue you and overtake you until you are destroyed, because you would not obey the Lord your God by keeping His commandments and His statutes which He commanded you (Deuteronomy 28:15, 43-45).

3

THE NEW DEAL

I have always been fascinated by history. I sometimes think I was born into the wrong century because there is little demand for historians in our generation. Today it seems that people are seeking prophets more than historians. And yet, the future becomes much clearer in the light of history. There are two old clichés that I appreciate very much: "Those who fail to learn from the past are doomed to repeat it." and "The more things change, the more they stay the same."

We think we generate new ideas, but in reality we only keep modifying some old ideas that previous generations thought they created. Such an idea was the New Deal.

Franklin Roosevelt was elected at the depth of the Depression, in 1932, based on a catchy slogan his party had adopted from the Republicans: "a chicken in every pot." Only this time, it would be a *government* chicken in every pot. The promise was to restore the American economy, no matter what the cost. It was a clear trade-off between the short-term needs of families in a depression and freedom from government controls. According to the interpretation of the Constitution at that time, there was simply no way that the federal government could give taxpayers' money to private individuals, no matter how justified it seemed. In order to get its agenda passed, the Roosevelt administration had to literally reinterpret the Constitution. The founding fathers had created a remarkable system of checks and balances that ensured that no short-term crisis could undermine the long-term rights of American citizens, even if the citizens wanted to do so, which clearly the thirties generation did.

The New Deal designers had a four-item agenda they wanted to implement:

1. Initiate direct transfers of payments (dubbed "entitlements") to Americans who needed help
2. Establish the federal government as an overseer and regulator of American business—particularly banking
3. Strengthen the strong central banking system to regulate all monetary policy
4. Establish a national depositors' insurance program.

Grover Cleveland best stated the prevailing policy. . . . "It is the responsibility of the citizens to support their government. It is not the responsibility of the government to support its citizens."

Taken individually, each of these ideas were radical enough but, collectively, they represented the most sweeping changes in America since the framing of the Constitution. Perhaps the president could have convinced the American people to amend the Constitution to allow these adaptations, but time did not permit the process. So he attempted to implement them through legislation—virtually all of which the Supreme Court ruled unconstitutional. This set off a six-year battle between the president and the court, which eventually ended with the replacement of the dissenting majority of the court by 1939.

In the meantime, the agenda went forward through the well-established political process known as "stonewalling." This is where Congress creates a law, which the president signs and implements, such as relief payments to farmers for farm price supports. The Supreme Court vetoes the law as unconstitutional, but since the funds have already been distributed, they cannot be recovered. Congress then passes another very similar law, which the president signs and implements. The new law is later vetoed by the court again. And so the process goes on year after year, until enough of the court is replaced that presidential policy becomes constitutionally acceptable. With no limit to the number of consecutive terms a president could serve, it was simply a matter of whether Roosevelt would outlive the older court members. He did.

Americans were dependent on the redistribution of taxpayers' funds by the federal government for the first time in our short democracy.

I would like to review briefly the agenda (policies) of the New Deal administration, because understanding these four policies is essential to understanding the future of our economy.

POLICY NUMBER 1:
ENTITLEMENTS

Perhaps President Grover Cleveland best stated the prevailing policy concerning transfer payments from the federal government to private citizens when he made his historic stand against helping a deserving orphanage in New York City during a severe economic crisis: "I will not be a party to stealing money from one group of citizens to give to another group of citizens; no matter what the need or apparent justification. Once the coffers of the federal government are open to the public, there will be no shutting them again." He went on to conclude, "It is the responsibility of the citizens to support their government. It is not the responsibility of the government to support its citizens."

In Cleveland's generation, another politician wrote, "A democracy is not a form of government to survive. For it will only succeed until its citizens discover they can vote themselves money from the Treasury, then they will bankrupt it." That politician was Karl Marx.

Under the New Deal, a variety of direct entitlement programs were started, including the Civilian Conservation Corps (CCC), in which citizens were employed by the federal government to work on public projects. These projects ranged all the way from one group digging holes that another group filled in to constructing hydroelectric dams.

In addition, the farm support program paid farmers to take certain crops out of production to raise the prices. Often farmers were paid to grow crops and then were required to plow them under in order to receive their subsidies.

Social Security was designed to ensure that all Americans had some retirement, disability, and survivors' death benefits.

By 1938 the federal government had transferred nearly $60 billion in revenues to the farmers, the unemployed, the retired, the sick, and sometimes lazy Americans. The first step of the New Deal was entrenched and irrevocable. Americans were dependent on the redistribution of taxpayers' funds by the federal government for the first time in our short democracy.

To be fair, I need to point out that some of the programs had great merit. Child labor was abolished, natural resources (such as the Colorado River and the Tennessee Valley) were developed, and a variety of other good programs were started. But many of these were already in progress before the New Deal arrived. Child labor was rapidly vanishing in the industrialized North and West simply because machines could do the jobs faster and cheaper. Several states already had efficient resource development projects underway when the Depression struck. They lacked the resources to continue the projects but would have done so after the Depression ended.

POLICY NUMBER 2:
GOVERNMENT REGULATIONS

For most Americans alive today, the idea that the federal government can force car companies to increase their gas mileage or install safety belts is totally acceptable. We also accept the policy that the Occupational Safety and Health Administration (OSHA) should inspect a business to ensure that it complies with federal standards for workers' safety. We accept the mandate of the Environmental Protection Agency (EPA) to require all businesses to meet federal environment standards. And the list goes on.

Certainly some of these federal agencies do a good job and provide a needed service, but the issue is really a broader one: Is this a legitimate role of our government? Prior to the New Deal, most Americans would have said emphatically, "No!"

Deciding where to draw that line is a difficult task. Few historians would disagree that the federal government did too little in the way of regulating the banks and stock market prior to the collapse in '29. But once that pendulum swings, it usually goes to the opposite extreme, as apparently it now has.

It is an interesting parallel that many of the same policies were being instituted in Germany at this time.

Roosevelt shut down all the banks and reopened them with strict federal controls, including federally insured deposits. From this base, the government branched out to touch virtually every business in America. Using cheap federal credit, the New Deal established controls over how many tractors were built, and at what price. Homes financed with federal monies had to be built according to the Federal Housing Authority's codes. Farmers who wouldn't join the land bank program found their credit cut off. Even states that didn't adopt federal standards for schools, roads, sewage, etc. were in jeopardy of having their supplemental federal funds cut off. Money became an effective social weapon to place the federal government at the top of all planning.

It is an interesting parallel that many of the same policies were being instituted in Germany at this time. The Nazis enforced their rule through force. The New Deal strategists enforced theirs through financial intimidation. The term "Fascist," which is normally applied to Nazi Germany, is equally applicable to the American economy. Fascism simply means "privately owned but centrally controlled."

POLICY NUMBER 3:
A CENTRAL BANK

President Woodrow Wilson had been successful in getting the Federal Reserve Banking Act passed into law; but in reality, it was little more than a paper system. The strong independent banks called the shots, and the Federal Reserve followed obediently. The New Deal changed all that. With virtually all the banks on the brink of collapse, President Roosevelt succeeded in establishing the Federal Reserve Board as the authority in banking. Independent banks were not forced to join the Federal Reserve System. But those that did not found they could not transact business through any member bank. Once the member banks' deposits were insured through the Federal Depositors Insurance Corporation (FDIC), the death of the nonaligned banks was just a matter of time.

Unfortunately, the same system that makes it possible for banks to multiply their deposits into loans also makes them vulnerable to defaults by borrowers.

With a strengthened Federal Reserve Banking system in place, the administration had a potent weapon to fight swings in the economy. The central bank could inflate the currency (the New

Deal also dropped the gold standard and made the ownership of gold illegal); it could reallocate funds to distressed areas through loans; and it could create money out of thin air through the use of "fractional banking."

Fractional banking is so fundamental to our later discussion of the coming economic earthquake, I would like to digress for a moment and give a brief overview of the fractional banking system.

The central bank (Federal Reserve) establishes a minimum reserve requirement for all member banks. This policy is meant to maintain a reserve in the central bank that can be used to help members when necessary. The money is loaned to members, who then can lend it to distressed citizens; at least that was the rationale behind it. Two factors become important in such a reserve system: the reserve requirement and the discount rate (the interest paid to the Reserve for members to borrow money). Requiring member banks to set aside reserves at no interest and then borrow from the reserves at interest would seem to be a difficult policy to sell, unless the system offered them something in return. Let's look at an example of how the Federal Reserve and "fractional banking" aids its members.

In our example, let's assume that the Fed (Federal Reserve) required member banks to deposit 10 percent of all their deposits with the central bank. Now let's assume that a member bank accepts a customer's deposit of $1,000. You would logically assume it would send 10 percent ($100) to the Fed. Right? Wrong. Instead, it sends the entire $1,000, representing assumed deposits of $10,000. The bank then lends an imaginary $9,000 to its customers.

Where did they get this money to lend? That's the function of the centralized system of "cooperating" banks. They don't actually have the money. Each member bank agrees to accept the "paper" of the other banks. So the loan is honored the same as cash when deposited. It works even better if the borrower deposits the "loan money" in the issuing bank. Each deposit becomes collateral for additional loans and member banks can lend as much as *700 percent* of actual cash deposits.

Unfortunately, the same system that makes it possible for banks to multiply their deposits into loans also makes them vulnerable to defaults by borrowers. With scant reserves, the banks must depend even more heavily on the central bank, further securing the system. Look around and see how many non-member banks survive today.

POLICY NUMBER 4:
NATIONAL DEPOSITORS' INSURANCE

As mentioned before, the benefits of a guaranteed depositors' insurance plan attracted many banks into the Federal Reserve System. It serves one more function that has a long-term detrimental effect on the whole economy. Depositors are less concerned about the lending policies of their banks.

Perhaps the leading opposition economist of the Roosevelt era was Dr. Ludwig Von Mises. Dr. Von Mises, having lived through the Depression in Germany after World War I, had seen the devastating effects of uncontrolled government "management" of the monetary system.

Von Mises states in his book, *Money, Method, and the Market System*: "Banks which promise (depositors) no more than they can fulfill without extraordinary assistance from the central bank never jeopardize the stability of the country's currency. . . . If the central banks did not believe it was their duty to cover up the consequences of the deposit banks' errors in lending, they could not jeopardize the assets of the prudent bankers."

There are many noted economists who believe the New Deal dealt the American economy a death blow that has taken nearly sixty years to surface fully.

Essentially, Von Mises said, and later proved, if the abuses get widespread enough, even the central bank (or the FDIC) cannot cover the losses. Ultimately the government will either inflate the currency to pay the bills or it will tax its citizens to do so. Since the government's ability to tax is limited to what the taxpayers will accept, it becomes politically more expedient to inflate the currency through debt accumulation.

Certainly what we have seen in the demise of the Savings and Loans associations testifies to this analysis. What we have not yet seen is the effect of billions (or trillions) of dollars of government debt coming due. The certainty is that no debt can be accumulated indefinitely. The compound interest curve eventually makes even the payment of interest impossible.

There are many noted economists who believe the New Deal dealt the American economy a death blow that has taken nearly sixty years to surface fully. We live in a highly regulated economy, run by people whose only claim to success is getting elected to a government office. No one can deny that federal entitlements programs are out of control. They consume more than 50 percent of all government spending now. A majority of Americans draw some form of direct or indirect government subsidy.

The central banking system now determines interest rates for virtually every bank in the country. A change in the reserve requirement or discount policy will affect the lives of every American, regardless of their economic status.

Government regulation has become so pervasive that between the EEOC, OSHA, EPA, IRS, and so on, no business escapes government interference. More and more businesses are being relocated to less controlled countries, with the resultant loss of millions of jobs in America. Often entire industries live or die according to the whims and wishes of officials who are not subject to any election, veto, or control by the citizens who pay their salaries.

The national bank insurance plan has been so abused that now taxpayers are being "asked" to cough up *thousands of dollars* each to pay for the S&L losses. This is the logical consequence of allowing a system to operate devoid of any local controls. Because their funds were "insured," depositors simply didn't know or care that their local S&L was making stupid loans, as well as helping many managers live like kings.

The seeds sown in the New Deal administration are still growing in our economy today. Once the process is started, it is very difficult to correct!

4

LIFE IN A DEPRESSION

The previous chapter gave a brief description of what the start of the Great Depression was like from inside the stock market. But that was only the beginning of a decade of economic hard times. It was the average American family who felt the real brunt of an economy that was plunged into the longest depression in U.S. history.

At one point, nearly 40 percent of all available workers were unemployed, causing a trauma so great it can only be grasped by those who lived it. America was a country without hope, at least economically. The middle class virtually disappeared. There were the rich who prospered through, and even because of, the depression; and there were the others who had lost everything.

To understand the impact of the Great Depression, we must return to the decade leading up to the collapse. This era was called the Roaring Twenties, appropriately named because society was roaring—both economically and socially.

Almost 70 percent of all Americans lived in rural communities that supported the farming industry. Agriculture was the primary business of America. For the most part, farmers were hard-working, family-oriented people whose social lives revolved around their churches. Elections were held in the church, politicians spoke to constituents there, even public schools met in church buildings. The vast majority of Americans believed in God, attended church regularly, and considered themselves to be moral, ethical people.

The successful conclusion of World War I established America as the world leader in virtually every category.

The same could not be said about all Americans though—especially those in the entertainment, political, or money-lending business. Often their lives revolved around gaudy shows, gross immorality, gangsters, and crooked politicians.

The successful conclusion of World War I established America as the world leader in virtually every category: economics, military, entertainment, and social "graces." The Vanderbilts, Carnegies, Morgans, and Kennedys became the socially elite, replacing the European gentry.

When Americans turned their energies toward producing goods, they simply out-produced the entire world. It was a time of unprecedented economic prosperity, led by a mechanized revolution in industry and agriculture. For the first time in the history of mankind, less than one-half of the working force could provide enough food for the majority and still have plenty left to export for sale. By the end of the twenties, farm efficiency had improved so greatly that only 20 percent of the working force was needed on the farms; 80 percent was freed to work in other areas of production.

In addition to being relieved from heavy labor and long hours on the farm, Americans were confronted with a plethora of new products. Automobiles were within the reach of average wage earners; homes were available on long-term financing (up to seven years); refrigerators, washing machines, radios, gas stoves, and the like were all flooding onto the market.

Credit cards were not yet invented, but consumer credit was readily available from willing merchants who knew that their friends and neighbors would pay their bills.

It was in this time of prosperity that the average savings rate of Americans declined from 12 percent of their incomes to less than 4 percent. The reason was twofold: There were many new products they wanted and no real need for pessimism about the future. The Republicans had originally coined the term "a chicken in every pot" to describe the prosperity that Americans were enjoying under their leadership.

The attitudes of the average American can be understood best by looking into the lives of a family who lived through this period of prosperity and the depression that followed.

The following story is based on past conversations with a personal friend. The narration is mine; the descriptions are his.

I had been working at the Ford Motor Company for nearly four years by 1929. Times were good in Detroit, and buyers flocked to the car showrooms every year as soon as the new models came out.

By 1929 old Henry (Ford) agreed that Ford buyers could have a choice of colors and style. Until 1925 Ford buyers could have any color they wanted, as long as it was black! But with Chevrolets outselling Fords, Mr. Ford had given in to his designers, who wanted to make several models and colors available. The change perked up the "A model" sales.

After renting for the first seven years of our marriage, Mary and I bought our first home. We had to finance nearly three thousand dollars, even after her father gave us a thousand dollars for the downpayment. I figured it would be worth it in the long run, though. The payments were nearly fifty dollars a month, which scared us both a little, but I had a good job and the money was budgeted. With car sales being so good, the plant was running double shifts, plus overtime. *After all*, I reasoned, *I work for one of the biggest companies in America, and prospects have never been better; why not buy a home?*

I kept reading about all the money being made in the stock market, and some of the other men on my shift had even borrowed money to invest. One of the guys, Bobby Thomas, bragged how he had made $600 in one month. Maybe he did, but he was known to exaggerate—a lot. Mary and I talked about investing, but she argued that we needed things for the house more than we needed stocks. I knew she was probably right, but it sure looked like an easier way to make money than working on an assembly line.

The last week in October 1929, I heard several of the men talking about how the stock market had dropped suddenly, and a lot of people feared it would drop some more. I had read about it in the papers—they called it the biggest drop in the history of the stock market—but I didn't think much about it then. After all, we didn't have any stocks, and Mr. Ford was so rich it surely couldn't affect him very much. The thing that did bother me was how much attention the stock market drop was getting around the plant. They made it sound like the end of the world might happen any day. When Mary seemed worried, I said, "Honey, even if people lose money in the stock market, I don't see what difference it makes. After all, they didn't have the money before the stocks went up, did they?"

"No, I guess you're right," she told me. But it still worried her. And deep inside, it worried me some too. I just didn't like things happening that I had no control over.

I was working first shift on Tuesday, when someone came racing into the plant yelling that the market had collapsed. In a few minutes the whole plant was buzzing about it. I wondered, *Why is everyone so upset because stock prices dropped?* So I asked Bobby Thomas. He said, "It means a lot of people are going to get wiped out." With that, he took his work apron off and left the plant.

Later I learned that he had borrowed a lot of money from his wife's parents, who were farmers, and he had lost it all. I never saw him again, because they packed up and moved to escape their creditors.

I left work that evening with a sense of dread like I had never felt before. From all the conversations I overheard, it was obvious that the stock market crash was going to affect more than just some stock investors. The evening papers made it sound like America had just lost a war. I began to realize that the comfort level I had felt just a week earlier was rapidly disappearing. Mary was pregnant with our third child and I didn't want to lose my job—not when we had just bought a home.

When I got home Mary was listening to the radio. "What does it mean?" she asked as soon as I walked in the door.

"I don't know," I told her. I was so mentally exhausted I just dropped into one of our well-worn chairs. I had stopped on the way home to pick up the "Extra" edition of the paper, which told all about the stock market crash. It read like the world was collapsing, right along with the stock market.

"Betty Alterman from my Sunday School class called and said she heard the banks are in trouble," Mary told me fretfully.

"I don't see how that's possible," I assured her. But the frown I must have been wearing didn't hide my inner feelings.

I hadn't even thought about the banks! I tried to visualize the large brick bank building and the massive safe that was protecting our money. *How could a bank fail just because of the stock market?* I asked myself. I didn't know the answer, but I wanted to avoid upsetting Mary, so I tried to hide what I was feeling.

"Do you think we should draw out our savings?" Mary asked me. I noticed her soft brown eyes were moist. "It's only sixty dollars, but it's all we have. I was going to use some of it to have the furniture recovered."

> *It had only been two weeks since the crash, and I was out of a job, had no money, and had a wife and two kids to feed.*

"There's just no way a big bank like First National could fold just because of a stock market problem," I told her confidently. "We're at least 650 miles from New York City, so how could it affect our bank here in Detroit?"

Little did I know at that time how wrong I was. Not only did the market crash affect our bank, it affected every bank in Detroit. As the situation worsened, reports of bank failures in New York panicked depositors all over the country. Within a few days lines formed outside every bank, waiting for them to open so people could get their money out.

President Hoover appealed to the public not to panic, and he assured Americans that the country was still "as sound as a dollar." But the lines still formed every day.

Finally I told Mary we should get our money out too. But I had waited a day too long, because the day Mary went to stand in line, the bank never opened its doors. A bank employee came out and told everyone the bank had run out of money and wouldn't be opening again.

"What's going to happen?" Mary asked as we lay in bed that evening, unable to sleep. "Every day things seem to get worse instead of better. Will you lose your job?"

"I don't know, honey," I answered as I tried to sort out what had happened in the last week. "Ford is a big company. I don't think it could be in trouble." But even as I tried to comfort Mary, I knew the awful truth: the whole country is in trouble.

The newspapers were full of reports of companies failing. There were even reports of rich people who had lost everything jumping out of windows.

The next Monday, when I went to work, our shift was told to wait before clocking in; the shift supervisor wanted to talk to us.

I had that feeling of dread again. I knew what he was going to say. We all did. We just hated to admit that it could happen to us. Two weeks ago we were working overtime to produce cars because the demand was so great, but in the last week orders had dropped off to nearly zero.

When the shift supervisor came out, he told us that our shift was being eliminated until the slowdown was over. That was bad enough, but then he said that the company was short on cash and we wouldn't be able to get our severance pay until later.

It had only been two weeks since the crash, and I was out of a job, had no money, and had a wife and two kids to feed. When I came home in the middle of the day, Mary guessed what had happened.

"You lost your job, didn't you?" she asked.

"Not really," I told her, trying to ease the burden some. "It's just that orders are down, so they're furloughing our shift. You know they've done that before."

Mary didn't say anything, but I knew I wasn't fooling her. She just turned back to her ironing. "What about your severance pay?" she asked without looking at me.

"The supervisor said it would be a little while before we could get it. He said the company is short on cash right now, but it shouldn't be too long." I added the last part even though I knew she wouldn't believe it any more than I did. I thought it might give her something to hang on to.

In the three weeks that followed, I looked everywhere for a job—any job. But there weren't any jobs in Detroit. Almost every business in the city was tied to the car companies, and when they slowed down, everything slowed down.

Our food supply dwindled and things got critical. We couldn't expect much help, even from our friends at church. Most of them were in the same fix as us, or worse. The pastor did set up a food pantry in the church where anyone who had extra could share with those who had needs, and thank God for that! At least we were able to eat, even if it meant eating mostly beans for a while. I still believed what was happening was temporary. *A whole country can't just shut down*, I kept telling myself.

For the next eight months, I hopped rides from one town to the next, looking for any kind of work. But everywhere I went there were a hundred men ahead of me.

We missed the next month's mortgage payment, and a week later we got a notice from the bank saying we needed to pay up or vacate the premises.

"How can the bank do that?" Mary asked me angrily. "We can't get our money out, but they can tell us to move out of our home?"

I wasn't sure how the bank could do that either, but since it wasn't open anymore I couldn't even talk to anyone about it. A week later a man knocked on the door. Handing me an eviction notice, he said if we didn't vacate within the week he would be back with the police to put us out.

"But where will we go?" I shouted at him through the screen door. "We don't have any money, and the bank is closed!"

"I can't help you, mister," he replied without emotion. "I just serve the papers for the court. You'll have to get a lawyer and talk to the judge."

I knew we couldn't do that. I didn't have enough money for bus fare, much less to pay a lawyer. So we packed up what we could carry and got ready to move.

The church had set up a temporary shelter because so many families had lost their homes. We stayed there for nearly three weeks, until another couple offered to let us stay with them. The husband worked for the railroad so he still had a job, although his pay had been cut in half.

I knew I had to find work, and there just wasn't any in Detroit, so I had to go where there was work. My problem was that I didn't have any money and no real prospects of getting any.

The railroad engineer we were staying with mentioned that a lot of men were hitching rides on box cars to search for work. He said the railroad officials had tried to stop them, but there were just too many. "As long as you don't get on or off in the rail yards, the engineers will look the other way," he said. The next day I hopped a ride on a south-bound freight. Someone had said there was work in Florida.

For the next eight months, I hopped rides from one town to the next, looking for any kind of work, but everywhere I went there were a hundred men ahead of me. Desperate men stood on street corners selling apples or begging just to feed their families.

I spent nights in makeshift camps with other men looking for work. Some had given up already and made their way by stealing what they could to survive. Being a Christian, I knew the Lord wouldn't approve of such things.

I picked up a few odd jobs here and there—enough to keep body and soul together but not enough to help Mary and our kids much (our third child had been born by then).

It was almost a year before I finally got a regular job as a gardener at a mansion in Palm Beach. It didn't pay much, but it did come with a small cottage (as the owner called it). A year earlier I would have called it a shack.

I lived like slaves must have lived a hundred years earlier. What money I made went mostly for food, with a little to send back to the family. I earned about thirty cents a day, when I was paid at all. I worked from sunup to sundown, keeping up the grounds of a politician's winter residence. Even now, I still remember that big house sitting empty most of the year, while I slept in a run-down shack, fighting off blood-thirsty mosquitoes.

If I could advise the younger generation, I'd say, "Believe only half of what you read about the economy and none of what you hear."

Finally in 1934 the economy in Florida had improved enough for me to get a job selling insurance door-to-door on commission. It amazed me how so many people I called on had plenty of money, when most families were living hand-to-mouth. Once I hit on the idea of convincing the rich that insurance was a way for them to protect their money against another crash, things started to go pretty well for me.

By 1936 I was able to bring Mary and the boys down to Florida. I decided it was time to give up my caretaker job. I had kept it even though I was making a pretty good living selling insurance. I guess the Depression had left such an impact on me that I hesitated to give up a sure job for one where I didn't know if I'd sell anything from day to day. But once I had some of those rich customers telling their friends about me, business really picked up.

To this day, I still remember the "hobo" camps where a bunch of us would sit around a fire and talk about the "good ol' days" when we had jobs. No matter how good things got in later years, I continued to remind myself how bad they had been and could be again, so I always tucked something away in a secret place. I never needed it, but I guess it's like a fire insurance policy; it's there, just in case. . . .

If I could advise the younger generation, I'd say, "Believe only half of what you read about the economy and none of what you hear." By the time my generation knew we had a problem, it was too late to do anything about it. We thought we had all the answers too, but what we found out was, when the chips were down, the politicians still had their jobs. We didn't.

Bill retired in 1973 after having operated a highly profitable insurance business for nearly forty years. Until his death in 1984, he was involved in a major effort to eliminate government waste and warn Americans about the dangers of excessive debt.

5

THE SEEDS OF DESTRUCTION

The Great Depression ended with the United States' entry into World War II. There is no evidence that the measures taken by the New Deal administration actually did anything to shorten the Depression. Obviously they did help the plight of Americans suffering from the effects of a decade-long depression. I believe history will reflect that the short-range benefits given to the thirties' generation were provided at the expense of future generations. There is one certainty: The function of the federal government as a provider was established permanently.

World War II provided the impetus to solidify the government's role as the nation's chief economic architect. For nearly four years Franklin Roosevelt was in total control of the country. Survival necessitated strong leadership, and Roosevelt was not one to shirk that role.

Coming out of the war, there was a tremendous need to reintegrate the GIs into American society without disrupting the entire economy. The plan that was instituted was dubbed the "GI Bill." This law empowered the government to provide college grants to servicemen (and women), fund new housing under the Veteran's Administration Loan Act, and expand business in Europe through the use of loans to both allies and former enemies through the Marshall Plan. The federal government went into the development business in a big way.

Perhaps the most significant economic change of the second half of the twentieth century was the discovery of instant prosperity (credit) by millions of American families.

Logically speaking, the debts incurred during the war should have been paid off immediately after the hostilities ended. But with the expanded role of government, the surpluses were diverted into expanding U.S. influence at home and abroad instead. With the expansion of the Farm Credit Bureau, the Small Business Administration, the Veteran's Administration, and others, the country prospered in an unprecedented postwar boom.

Billions went into educating GIs and their spouses, as well as providing low-interest loans to house them. As the FHA program was expanded to provide low-cost financing to nonveterans, America went on a building boom. No one questioned the wisdom of the government-backed expansion. After all, taxes were low, interest rates were low, inflation was a modest one-half percent per year, and, except for a brief recession in 1948, business was booming. Eisenhower was elected president and Americans thought prosperity was their God-given heritage.

Perhaps the most significant economic change of the second half of the twentieth century was the discovery of instant prosperity (called credit) by millions of American families. Since the Great Depression, most Americans had been weaned from the use of credit: some because of bitter memories, others because the bankers simply knew better than to lend money to people who could ill-afford it. Credit was available during the fifties but was limited primarily to home mortgages and some short-term car loans. During the sixties, loans for almost everything—from college tuition to television sets—burst onto the scene.

The federal government, after running budget surpluses or only slight deficits during most of the Eisenhower administration, began its disastrous experiment with massive entitlement programs.

In his famous inaugural address, President Kennedy said, "Ask not what your country can do for you. . . ." At that time those with their hands in Uncle Sam's pockets numbered *only* about twenty-two million. In the next decade, that number would swell to almost 160 million.

President Lyndon Johnson was consumed by two strategies that would prove to be the most costly in American history: the protection of South Vietnam and massive federal transfers to the "war on poverty."

Perhaps the economy could have absorbed either of these at any given time. We were, after all, the most prosperous nation on earth, with a trade surplus in almost every area of business. But not even the U.S. economy could swallow $100 billion of war costs and nearly $500 billion in welfare transfers in a five-year period without either some sizable tax increases or huge deficits. The federal government opted to increase both.

In the early sixties, average-income families paid about 7 percent of their income in direct taxes. They also spent about 15 percent of their disposable income on interest payments (primarily home mortgages).

By 1969 they were paying 14 percent of their incomes in taxes and spending 22 percent on interest. The amounts were still manageable but growing faster than incomes.

In 1963 the federal government collected approximately $107 billion in income taxes. By 1970 it was collecting more than $187 billion, an increase of some 42 percent, while incomes went up an average of 12 percent. Still, things weren't all that bad economically for most Americans. There were periodic bouts with recession but, essentially, the period from 1961 to 1970 was the longest sustained period of economic growth in the history of the nation.

By the late sixties, many Americans who had lived through the Great Depression were leaving the work force and retiring to a stable, relatively noninflationary economy.

If the debt had been dealt with swiftly and aggressively, it could have been controlled or even eliminated. But Americans had no such mentality in the seventies; nor did their elected officials.

Interest rates had risen from approximately 4 percent in 1960 to about 6 percent by 1970—nothing to be alarmed about for the average home buyer. Besides, the "baby boomers" of the postwar era were coming into the mainstream, and they needed homes and cars, as well as a variety of other consumer goods. The sixties may have been tumultuous times politically, but economically the country was still on a roll.

A few prophets of doom continued the warnings about too much debt and too much government in the economy; but in large part, their warnings fell on deaf ears. Poverty was due to be eliminated by the mid-seventies; people were bored by men on the moon; and Watergate had not yet tarnished President Nixon's administration.

THE SEVENTIES

What few Americans realized was that the seeds from the New Deal were just beginning to germinate in the economy. The aggregate national debt had grown from $22 billion in 1932 to just under $400 billion by 1970. By 1979 the debt had more than doubled to $829 billion.

The difficulty with a debt that doubles in ten years is that the interest compounds to the point that it can no longer be paid out of current revenues. Once the interest itself is debt financed, the compounding accelerates.

If the debt had been dealt with swiftly and aggressively, it could have been controlled or even eliminated. But Americans had no such mentality in the seventies; nor did their elected officials. Tax revenues could never sustain the level of growth Americans were used to—not and still fulfill the Great Society's goals too. So by 1970 the die was cast for a debt-run economy in which the deficits of the past would seem minuscule in comparison. Instead of millions, we would hear of a deficit in the billions. Later the billions would aggregate to trillions.

Perhaps it would be helpful to use an analogy to the amounts of money we're discussing.

- A *million* dollars in tightly bound $1,000 bills would produce a stack four inches high.
- A *billion* dollars in tightly bound $1,000 bills would produce a stack about three hundred feet high.
- A *trillion* dollars in tightly bound $1,000 bills would produce a stack nearly *sixty-three miles* high!

Sometimes it's too easy to lose sight of what some of these numbers really mean. With a budget deficit of only $3 billion in 1970, the Federal government went on a debt-funded spending binge. This was not to combat a depression or to oppose an invading army. It was a social experiment run amok with most Americans eventually taking some form of government subsidy. We were literally mortgaging future generations to feed our indulgences. The traditional family suffered greatly as mothers went to work to help fund the family's debt and tax payments. The great wealth transfers of the 1920s were under way once again. Only this time even the federal government would mortgage the country.

Government strategies of the seventies failed to take into account two critical factors: the deficits would eventually translate into higher inflation and the compounding interest on the national debt would create even greater deficits.

The total federal debt increased by approximately $35 billion from 1950 to 1960 and by $90 billion from 1960 to 1970. But it would climb by more than *$500 billion* by 1980! But I'm getting ahead of myself in the logical progression of our economy.

In a futile attempt to control the "rampant" inflation of 1971 (4.4 percent), President Nixon ordered wage and price controls on the economy. No sooner were the controls in place than the political "negotiating" began. Those groups with the most lobbyists, or the biggest campaign contributors, began to receive special consideration. Within a few months, the only controls remaining were on the wages of average Americans. Eventually the controls were dropped altogether.

Then in 1973, the Arab oil embargo shocked most Americans into the realization that we were vulnerable too. Gas prices increased dramatically, climbing from forty cents per gallon to just over ninety cents, paving the way for the fuel-efficient Japanese cars to reach into the American market in a big way.

Prices of virtually all consumer items inflated rapidly. It was as if the pent-up prices from the earlier controls broke loose and swept aside everything in their wake. Our nation started a spending binge that paralleled that of the 1910-to-1920 era; only this time it was amplified by the government's deficit spending as well.

Inflation creates a unique attitude in most people: a buy-now mentality.

During the four years of the Carter administration, the national debt increased by nearly $250 billion—an unparalleled amount prior to that time. But also inflation roared to life, sending price increases into the double digits annually. Here we get a brief but revealing glimpse at a hyperinflationary economy in the U.S.

By early 1979, inflation was running at nearly 12 percent per year. This was relatively minor compared to many other industrialized nations at that time. Israel's inflation rate was nearly 80 percent; England's was 20+ percent; Germany's was as high as 30 percent. But in the U.S. we were used to spending what we wanted with little or no economic consequences. Americans responded to double-digit inflation by demanding that the government do something about it.

The primary tool the administration decided to use to combat inflation was a decrease in the money supply. Not wishing to repeat the mistakes of the Nixon administration with wage and price controls, President Carter had few other choices.

The method by which the Federal Reserve manipulates the available money supply is either an increase or decrease in the amount of credit available. To reduce the money supply, the Fed raises interest rates, which makes borrowing more costly. As the cost of credit goes up, more and more potential borrowers drop out. Since we are an economy run almost exclusively on credit now, consumer buying slows and, hopefully, so does inflation. This was one of the controls established during the Roosevelt era.

In spite of all the "controls" installed by the New Deal, the primary steering mechanism in the economy still remains public confidence. Unfortunately, the public had lost its confidence in the Carter administration because of several politically devastating events: the Panama Canal treaty, the Iranian hostage situation, and the Vietnam war legacy that President Carter inherited.

As a result, the only real effect the increased interest rates had was a slowdown in economic growth. The economy entered a new phase not seen before—"stagflation": a condition in which the economy is stagnant while inflation is still rising. Effectively we got the worst of two worlds—inflation and recession.

Inflation creates a unique attitude in most people: a buy-now mentality. As the value of their money declines, consumers are motivated to buy commodities before the prices go higher. Young couples see their dream homes slipping away, so they extend beyond what normally would be prudent to buy that home. Investors see their paper assets eroding, so they rush out to buy "real" assets, such as land, buildings, precious metals, and the like.

The late seventies and early eighties were such times. Almost anything that could be used as an inflation hedge was purchased. People who should have known better were buying assets at greatly inflated values, believing that inflation was here to stay.

I need to digress again to explain something about inflation. Inflation is caused by one primary factor: an artificial increase in the money supply. Higher prices in an economy are a symptom, not the problem.

Allow me to illustrate. If all currency were tied to a fixed asset, such as gold, no additional money could be circulated without an equivalent increase in the amount of gold held in reserve. Since gold is relatively scarce and costly to mine, it cannot be increased rapidly. Therefore, the total currency in circulation is relatively constant when tied to the gold supply.

Individual commodities, such as coffee, can go up in price because of demand, but with a fixed amount of currency in circulation, if coffee goes up in price, something else must come down. In other words, consumers must make a choice of buying coffee at the sacrifice of some other commodity, such as sugar. Overall there is no increase in commodity prices; hence, no inflation.

Obviously there can be gradual price increases as the supply of gold is expanded, but these would be long-term, not sudden, increases.

But take the currency off of any fixed commodity standard and see what can happen. Let's assume that the amount of currency available is regulated only by the wishes of a small group of economists who regularly put more money into circulation as they deem it necessary to keep the economy stimulated (as is true with the Fed).

Now suppose the price of coffee goes up as consumers discover its great merits. But instead of allowing another commodity (sugar in our previous example) to decrease (because sugar is produced in the district of an influential congressman), the Fed simply creates more money to fund the increased price of coffee.

The result is an overall price increase in the economy that is more or less permanent. The "more or less" is determined by whether or not the Fed makes the currency expansion permanent.

Obviously the mechanics by which our currency is inflated is more complex than I presented, but I trust you can see the big picture.

Inflation of the money supply is precisely why the New Deal administration removed our money from the gold standard and, later, the use of base metal coins was substituted for silver coins. The government economists now have created a mechanism whereby they can regulate the currency as they deem necessary. The result? Inflation.

WHY INFLATION DECLINED IN THE EIGHTIES

Actually, inflation did not decline in the eighties; it simply resumed the regular upward trend established before the rampant price increases of the seventies.

When Ronald Reagan became president, he brought into the office something that had been lacking in the previous three administrations: confidence. His programs were innovative (to be sure), and he was an eloquent orator. Simply put, Americans (in general) trusted his leadership.

What makes our government's debt so dangerous is that we are in debt beyond our total asset value. In other words, we are actuarily broke.

As a result, the tough measures he adopted to choke off inflation were accepted as necessary. Also, since most Americans had confidence in his ability to do what he said, they lowered their panic level and stopped the run on real assets. Inflation quieted down to a mere 6 percent per year. What would have been unthinkable inflation in 1960 became "the good ol' days" in 1984.

"Reaganomics" instituted sweeping tax cuts, particularly for the upper-income taxpayers. The Reagan advisers assessed (correctly I believe) that more money in the hands of those with a surplus would be reinvested in the economy. The U.S. economy boomed for nearly eight years, but President Reagan left the White House having bloated our economy with debt. The largest deficits in the history of any economy (more than $1.5 *trillion*) were accumulated during the longest period of uninterrupted economic growth.

THE X FACTOR: DEBT

The one factor we have not discussed yet is the three-dimensional aspect of our debt. We often think of "the debt" only in terms of our government when, in reality, that is one side of the three-sided debt issue: federal, consumer, and state.

THE NATIONAL DEBT

It is not new for our government or any other to borrow money. Most governments do so when in a crisis, such as a war. What is unique today is that our government borrows during good times and bad, during war and peace alike. But what makes our government's debt so dangerous is that we are in debt beyond our total asset value. In other words, we are actuarily broke.

*The average taxpayer's
"contribution" to the federal budget
(based on annual income of $38,000)
operates our government for
approximately one seventh of one second.*

Unfortunately, there seems to be no thought of ever trying to repay the debt. In truth, our government cannot even pay the *interest* on its debt, unless it does so through additional borrowing. The media present countries like Mexico, Brazil, and Argentina as so-called "banana" republics because they must borrow to pay the interest on their debts. But who would have ever believed this was possible for the world's largest economy?

The following graph shows the growth of the federal debt since 1960, with projections through the year 2004. Anyone who reads this graph and is not alarmed by the economic consequences for our nation should enroll in Economics 101.

Growth of the Federal Debt

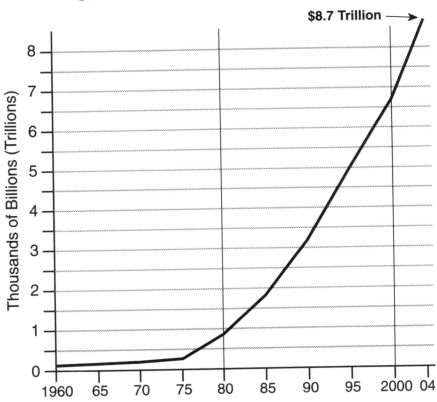

$8.7 Trillion →

Source: Department of the Treasury, Congressional Budget Office
Note: Projections after 1999 are extrapolated from CBO data.

I personally believe these estimates to be on the conservative side. When interest rates go up, these deficit projections will be out of date overnight. It is very possible that the federal debt could reach $10 trillion by the year 2004. At an interest rate of just 10 percent, Americans would be paying $1 trillion a year in interest!

In 1993 gross interest payments consumed 57 percent of all revenues from individual income taxes. And in 1993 on-budget federal spending was one trillion, one hundred forty-two billion dollars ($1,142,000,000,000). In addition, the government spent nearly another two hundred sixty-six billion ($266,000,000,000) in "off-budget" expenditures. Such figures tend to lose their significance to most of us, so let's put it in manageable "bites." At this spending level the federal government spends $3.86 billion a day! That amounts to $161 million an hour, or $2.68 million every minute, day and night. The average taxpayer's "contribution" to the federal budget (based on an annual income of $38,000) operates our government for approximately one-seventh of one second. Think about that the next time you read about how the government spends *our* money.

In l960 the average taxpayer worked 36 days to pay all of his or her taxes. In 1993, it took 123 days.

In order for the government to continue to operate, it must either cut spending, increase revenues, or find another "fix." I believe it is this other "fix" that represents danger to our economy, as I will demonstrate later.

CONSUMER DEBT

As dramatic as the increase in the national debt has been since the depression years, it pales in comparison to the increase in consumer debt. Americans are literally consuming their asset base and transferring their wealth to the lenders.

As we saw in the latter stages before the Great Depression, there was a massive transfer of wealth via debt to lenders. Today there is an even more massive transfer of wealth leaving the country. This is more ominous since the transfers often come back in the form of foreign ownership of American businesses. In 1983 the Japanese invested $1 billion in the U.S. In 1985 they invested $6.5 billion. In 1986 it was $12 billion. In 1990 their investments were estimated to be $65 billion.

Right now, foreign loans account for about 18 to 20 percent of our public debt.

Americans are living in an inflated economy created by the use of borrowed money. Since the early sixties, virtually all major assets have been purchased on credit. Since the mid-seventies, even consumer goods have been acquired on credit via the use of credit cards and equity loans.

Most American families, in spite of their outward appearance of affluence, live on the brink of economic disaster. They have little or no savings to fall back on in difficult times and now are borrowing against the equity in their homes to buy nonessential goods. If the value of their homes falls during an economic downturn, both the borrowers and the lenders are going to be in real trouble. The following graph gives a picture of where the average American is economically.

Outstanding Household Debt Relative to Disposable Personal Income 1973-1992

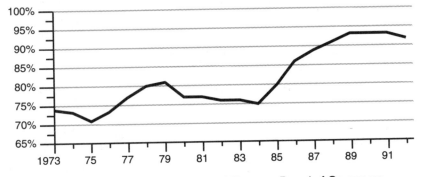

Source: Commerce Department, Federal Reserve Board of Governors

As you can see, the ratio of household debt to disposable income rose dramatically after 1983. Simply put, many Americans borrowed their way into prosperity.

The next graph demonstrates even more dramatically the trend in consumer borrowing. Americans are rapidly consuming all their available equity.

Home Mortgage Debt and Consumer Installment Debt Relative to Disposable Personal Income, 1972-1992

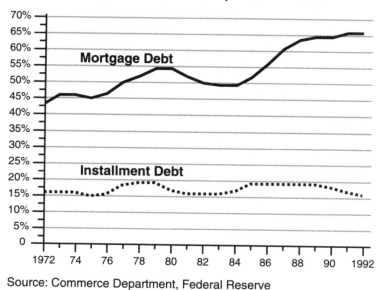

Source: Commerce Department, Federal Reserve

The graph on the next page indicates the source of the money that has funded the credit binge of the eighties (and nineties). Americans were persuaded to use their last source of available equity: their homes. When the tax laws were changed in 1986 to disallow interest deductions on all but home loans, the shift to equity lines of credit was clearly evident. One has to wonder if the law was changed specifically for this purpose. Without a new line of credit, the economy might well have slowed dramatically. The question is: Where will the next financial "rabbit" come from?

STATE DEBT

Anyone who reads the newspapers or watches the evening news knows that many states are in severe financial trouble. The same abuses that we see at the federal level are evident on a smaller scale at the state (and local) level. It is astounding to hear of state debts in the billions of dollars. It is even more astounding to hear about cities (like New York and Boston) with debts in the billions.

Home Equity Debt Outstanding 1987-1991

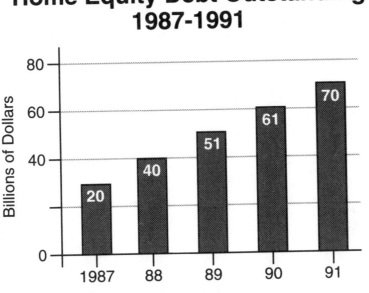

Source: Federal Reserve Board of Governors

It's as if the whole public system has gone insane. There is virtually no way these state governments can sustain such huge debts, and there is no "politically acceptable" way to repay them. With the taxpayers already struggling financially, higher taxes will push them to the brink of disaster, economically and emotionally.

Bear in mind that all of the debts owed by state and local governments are loans made by people who live off the proceeds. If these governments default, the ripple will be felt throughout the economy. With our economy teetering on the edge of disaster already, any ripple could swamp it. Any economy lives or dies on the basis of public confidence. Lose that confidence, and the system crashes.

As the graph on the next page demonstrates, the growth of nonfederal public debt has reached the epidemic level. We will certainly see many municipalities, and perhaps even some states, appealing to the courts for bankruptcy protection. That will be an interesting study in constitutional law—to see if the federal bankruptcy act extends to local governments.

Growth of State and Local Government Debt 1972-1991

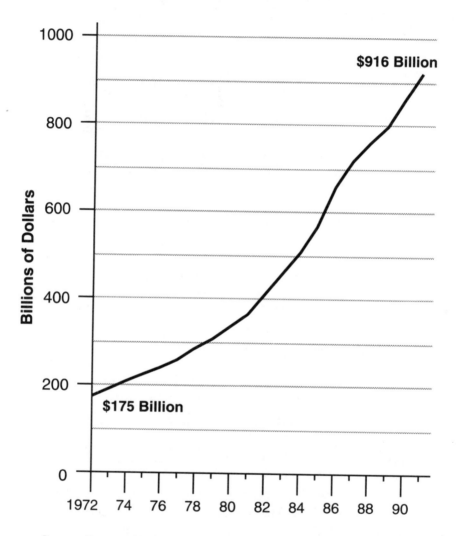

$916 Billion

$175 Billion

Source: Bureau of the Census

WHAT'S NEXT?

I trust that I neither bored you nor panicked you with all the details on debt in America, but it is the key to understanding the future direction of our economy.

As I said earlier, those who fail to learn from the past are doomed to repeat it. You'd think that just a little more than six decades after the most severe depression in U.S. history, we would remember the lessons learned: you can't spend more than you make forever and not pay the price, and when the bottom falls out it is the *lenders* who will be protected, not the *borrowers*.

God's Word gives us a clear indication that this principle has endured for more than three thousand years. For as Proverbs 22:7 says, *"The rich rules over the poor, and the borrower becomes the lender's slave."*

6

GERMANY AND ARGENTINA: EXAMPLES TO AVOID

THE LESSONS OF GERMANY

As a history buff, I try to recognize parallels between past events and current trends. At first glance, the parallels between 1990 America and 1918 Germany may not be obvious, but I believe there are many.

Germany, before the humiliating defeat in Europe, had an economy that was the envy of all Europe. However, after World War I, in the wake of the treaty at Versailles, the German government was required to make economic reparations to her European neighbors. To do so required transferring most of Germany's gold reserves to France and England. That left the German deutschemark (called reichsmark from 1925 to 1948) virtually stripped of any hard currency to support it.

Additionally, Germany had chronic unemployment because so much of her industry had been dismantled and removed to France and Belgium after the war. The government was put in the compromising position of finding it necessary to support the unemployed or risk rebellion in the cities during a very difficult economic time. This required a sizeable portion of the German budget to be siphoned off into transfer payments at a time when the government could least afford it.

> *The "enlightened" philosophy was that currency should not be linked to precious metals anyway, since it allowed for no direct government control over the economy. This philosophy would eventually resurface in America during the "New Deal."*

The debt payments to England and France for the war damage further stripped the country of needed operating capital, and Germany's main creditor, France, refused to budge on required payments. As one of the Proverbs says, "so the rich rule over the poor." Germany was faced with making some tough economic decisions, including the cessation of transfer payments (what we now call entitlements).

Instead, the government took the easier path of "monetizing" their currency. *Monetizing* is a polite economic term that means creating fiat (phony) money—sometimes called "funny money."

When the German government made the decision to print the money it needed, it was hailed by progressive economists as an enlightened move. The "enlightened" philosophy was that currency should not be linked to precious metals anyway, since it allowed for no direct government control over the economy. This philosophy would eventually resurface in America during the "New Deal."

It was assumed that by injecting a modest amount of new currency into the economy, only a modest amount of inflation would follow. Advocates of this plan assured the government leaders that a modest amount of inflation would be manageable and would actually allow producers to reap more profits, thus helping to repay the country's debts with cheaper currency.

When the decision to print unsupported money was made, the value of the German currency was approximately four marks to the dollar. Almost immediately the currency was devalued to about nine marks per dollar, achieving the economists' desired effect: German exports were suddenly more competitive, and debts were effectively cut in half by inflation.

Inside Germany it was another matter altogether. Suddenly creditors saw their loans reduced by half, along with their buying power. They lobbied the government for equalization— meaning that all loans should be indexed to the devalued mark.

When a loan is indexed, it requires that the principal amount be increased by the rate of inflation (much as Social Security payments are now). So if the currency is devalued by 50 percent, outstanding loans double in value. This has the effect of passing the burden along to the borrowers, instead of the lenders.

The request was initially rejected, and effectively all debts, internal and external, were cut in half. All new lending in Germany ceased at this point. No lender was willing to risk another devaluation and lose a sizeable portion of his equity to inflation.

What had seemed like a windfall to the debtors soon became a nightmare. The Allies (with the exception of England) demanded that Germany pay its war debts in kind (real goods), rather than with the devalued German currency. To guarantee this, France occupied a portion of the Ruhr coal mining district. Coal was Germany's main export, and France was determined to get its fair share. Instead, German workers declared a passive strike, effectively cutting off Germany's only source of foreign currency.

To compensate for the lack of currency, the Reichsbank (the German equivalent of our Federal Reserve) authorized the printing of more currency. This would prove to be the downfall of the German economy and, ultimately, the Republic.

As I commented previously, when any government makes the decision to inflate its economy through debt, eventually it will be faced with more difficult decisions about how to repay that debt. As long as the debt is held by its own people, the solutions are somewhat easier because it is in their interests to maintain the system. When the debt is held by foreigners, however, there is no choice but to either pay up or risk losing the ability to trade with other nations. Inevitably the government is faced with three basic choices: default, raise taxes, or inflate the currency.

Germany could not easily raise taxes since a large portion of its population was out of work, and a default would mean economic disaster. So, against the warnings of economists like Dr. Ludwig Von Mises, the government chose to inflate.

Immediately the currency rate fell from 8.9 marks per dollar to 191 marks to the dollar. Inside Germany this devaluation effectively wiped out all the creditors. In addition, retirees who held government or bank bonds saw their assets devalued by 2000 percent in one day!

Once the cycle started, it was virtually impossible to control. The government overseers authorized the printing of more currency to compensate for the devaluation. At the same time, they attempted to establish price controls within Germany to help stabilize the economy. The effect was to punish the working class, while many of the industrialists shifted to the black market to sell their goods at much higher prices. And since most of these sales went untaxed, this further reduced the federal revenues.

The net result of hyperinflation was the dissolution of the German government.

In June of 1922 the currency rate dropped to 350 marks per dollar. By October it was 4,500 per dollar. Prices were changing so rapidly in the stores that merchants adopted an indexing system. The prices on the goods, which might be several days old, were multiplied by the devalued mark. For example, a can of beans with a price of 10 marks stamped on it would be indexed by a factor of 30, making the current price 300 marks. As the currency prices changed, so did the food prices—about every minute or so! Within a few months an equivalent can of beans would sell for more than one million marks!

Once hyperinflation struck Germany, bank loans were indexed to the currency devaluation. But since wages were not indexed, the loans escalated far beyond the average worker's ability to repay them. Most average-income workers lost everything they owned. This massive shift of wealth would later pave the way for the National Socialist German Worker's Party (Nazis) to grasp power. The wealthy got wealthier, and the middle class got wiped out.

By January of 1923 the exchange rate was 18,000 marks per dollar. Prices changed while customers stood in long check-out lines. All the merchandise was cleaned out of the stores as soon as it was unloaded. In anticipation of the higher prices when they reordered, merchants would often mark their goods up several thousand percent higher than the "legal" daily limit.

Even so, it was not enough, and many small merchants failed, leaving the struggling, average-income workers with no place to buy except the black market, where a loaf of bread might sell for 100,000 marks—the equivalent of a month's wages at the time.

By October the currency exchange rate fell to 4.2 *trillion* marks per dollar! The deutschemark became worthless. Lifetimes of savings were wiped out, and the only form of trade for most Germans was barter. The mark became so worthless that the paper it was printed on was actually more valuable than the currency itself. So, instead of printing more currency, the Reichsbank simply issued stamps that could be pasted over existing bills.

I have a 1923 German bill that began with a value of 10,000 marks. The last stamp applied revalued it to three billion marks!

The net result of hyperinflation was the dissolution of the German government. After the collapse of the economy, Germans turned to socialism, believing that the free-enterprise system had failed them. When the depression of 1929 struck, Germany still had not recovered from the devastating effects of the earlier collapse. An obscure ex-Army corporal by the name of Adolf Hitler took over the government with the promise of "economic prosperity."

ARGENTINA: A MORE RECENT EXAMPLE

Often Americans think of Argentina as a small South American country whose economy is based mainly on ranching. But in

1940 Argentina was one of the world's fastest developing countries. In fact, it was the fifth largest exporter in the world. It was (and is) a country with great natural resources and the potential to become a world leader.

The example of Argentina is a study in what *not* to do to an economy. The Argentine leaders were greatly influenced by American economists who followed the theory known as Keynesian Economics. To refresh your memory, this is the philosophy that the central government should control the economy for the "good" of the workers. To implement Keynesian economics requires both a strong central monetary system, such as the Federal Reserve, and the ability to inflate the currency when necessary.

> *Most bureaucracies operate on the old formula of "more money in—more money out."*

In the early seventies Argentina, as well as many other developing countries, went on an aggressive modernization program, hoping to regain its pre–World War II status. To do so the Argentine government borrowed huge sums of money from foreign banks, especially those in the United States.

By 1980 their debt was $44 billion—nearly matching their GNP and requiring half of the government's income just to service the interest on the debt. Each successive year required more loans to keep the interest payments current. By the mid-eighties the international loan market began to dry up as lenders sensed a pending Argentine default. The Argentine government was faced with three choices: default, raise taxes, or inflate the currency.

As with most politicians who have sold their people on the role of the government as "the great provider," it is very difficult to pare back. In our country the politicians might face an angry electorate. In Argentina they might well have faced a firing squad.

If Argentina had simply defaulted on its debts, virtually all access to any additional loans would have been cut off. With an economy just beginning to emerge again, that would have resulted in some severe and immediate cutbacks. Perhaps in the long run, that track would have been better for the people, but few politicians operate in the "long run" today, so that option was discarded.

The second option of tax increases (and spending cutbacks) would seem the most logical approach. After all, that's what is expected of individuals when they overspend their own budgets, isn't it? But Argentina already had a tax rate of over 40 percent and a government that was spending money faster than the people could make it. Most bureaucracies operate on the old formula of "more money in—more money out."

Instead, the Argentine government, just as the Germans did some sixty years earlier, opted for the easy way out and began to inflate its currency. Simply put, they printed the money they needed.

In December 1989, to compensate for the new money that was being printed, the government devalued the Argentine currency (the austral) by 35 percent. On the black market, however, the austral dropped by an additional 50 percent, reflecting its true value. The official government valuation was 950 australs to the dollar; the rate anyone would actually accept was 1,500, but even that wouldn't last very long.

The government estimated that inflation would increase about 20 percent as a result of their actions. Instead it rose by nearly 700 percent! The middle class in Argentina was rapidly being wiped out. Retirees, pensioners, and those living on fixed incomes were destitute in less than a month.

In an effort to control the rampant inflation, the government froze prices on public services such as buses, hospitals, and utilities. But to cover the rising costs of imported goods, they had to print more money.

Within six months of printing the first currency, inflation accelerated to just under 100 percent per month! That meant the average Argentinean lost half of his buying power every single month. Before another six months had passed, the people of Argentina would look back on those times as "the good ol' days."

Prices in the open air markets of Buenos Aires soared as much as 100 percent *daily* as Argentineans rushed to buy all available food, anticipating greater inflation. Within one year of printing the first worthless currency, all savings were wiped out, and the only possible form of trade was barter (or dollars, which were illegal to own then). The Argentine economy was collapsing, and no other country would accept australs in payment for anything.

To encourage Argentineans to "save" and not convert their money into dollars on the black market, banks were directed to raise their interest rates to 600 percent per year. But with the annual inflation rate estimated at 2,000 percent, the interest hike did little to entice those with surpluses to leave them in the banks. There was a hemorrhage of assets leaving Argentina for other countries as the wealthy traded land, businesses, and whatever else they had for foreign currency. Land speculators were doing a booming business with wealthy Argentineans until they discovered that they were trading real assets for worthless paper. They quickly shifted their strategy, selling the land to foreign investors who would pay in other currencies.

One of the economic possibilities for the United States studied by the Grace Commission was that of hyperinflation.

By January of 1990 the annualized inflation rate was about 5,600 percent. Prices tripled while Argentineans slept. Millions were made in one black market trade, and then lost on the next one. That didn't provide much of an incentive to save. An American businessman visiting Argentina asked his Argentine counterpart if he should take a cab or a bus to their luncheon. "Take a cab," his associate quipped. "You don't have to pay until you get there, so it's cheaper." That mentality was more than just a joke in Argentina. All paper currency was converted into real assets as quickly as possible.

In an effort to gain at least some degree of control over inflation, the government (at the insistence of the World Bank) established the equivalent of martial law over the economy. The currency was frozen and the printing of any new money was forbidden; wages and prices were frozen; black marketing was punishable by long prison sentences; and so on. This helped to establish some semblance of sanity in an insane system, and by early 1991 inflation was reduced to 300 percent per year.

SWIFT INFLATION

Inflation does not have to creep into an economy, as the examples of both Argentina and Brazil demonstrate. When Argentina's annual budget deficit rose from 5 percent of their gross national product (about where the United States was in 1993) to 8 percent, inflation jumped from 4 percent per month to over 50 percent— in less than one year!

In Brazil, when the annual budget deficit reached 8 percent of the GNP, the inflation rate jumped from about 15 percent per month (considered modest in South America) to nearly 150 percent per month—in 3 days!

In 1984 President Reagan commissioned a panel of private citizens to review the federal budget and make recommendations on how to reduce the deficits. The study, under the direction of J. Peter Grace, was dubbed the Grace Commission. I will refer to that commission's report in subsequent chapters because it clearly reveals our economy's present and future conditions. One of the economic possibilities for the United States studied by the Grace Commission was that of hyperinflation. To get an accurate picture of what sparks hyperinflation (annual price increases of at least three digits), a committee selected by the Grace Commission did an extensive study of inflation in other countries. One of the principal figures in this study was Harry E. Figgie, Jr., chairman and chief executive officer of Figgie International, Inc., and a world-renowned industrialist. Mr. Figgie later wrote the best-selling book, *Bankruptcy 1995.*

While visiting Brazil, Argentina, Mexico, and Bolivia to evaluate their hyperinflation, Mr. Figgie was struck by the similar comments made by the more conservative members of their monetary policy groups.

In effect they all said something very similar: "What's wrong with the United States? You are on the same course that we were on—just several years behind us. Everything that we did wrong, you are doing wrong—only on a bigger scale. You have big budget deficits. You have a deficit in your balance of payments. You have allowed confidence in your currency to be eroded. You are dependent on foreign loans. You blame outsiders for your problems. Your businessmen call for more protectionism. And the exchange value of your currency is falling."

Their final comment to Mr. Figgie was, "Can't you tell your government to stop this madness before it's too late?"

Mr. Figgie's reply was, "I sure do hope so."

That was in 1985. Nearly a decade later our debt is much bigger, our balance of payments is worse, and our government has yet to implement more than a token amount of the Grace Commission's suggestions.

Mr. Figgie had an ominous word for Americans when he spoke before the League of Women Voters in July of 1990:

> There's never been a more critical time in our country than right now. There's never been a more critical issue than our budget deficits.
>
> This isn't a Democratic issue and it isn't a Republican issue. It's an American issue. We have perhaps five years left to deal with this problem through taxation and spending cuts, or we will pay the price others have paid. . . .

This is an ominous warning from a respected businessman who has no political "axe to grind." Later we will review some of the Grace Commission's more revealing predictions for the future of our economy.

It is interesting to note that many members of the Commission, as well as the report itself, came under great criticism by the economic liberals in Congress. The Commission members, who served at their own expense and paid all of their own staff, and whose committees were equally represented by Democrats and Republicans, were often accused of "partisan" politics—a term perfected in our Congress.

7

CYCLES OF DEPRESSION

Much has been written about economic cycles in America. Some economists have even suggested that the cycles are so predictable they can be relied upon to a high degree for most economic planning.

Perhaps the most well-known of the twentieth-century cycle theorists was Russian economist N.D. Kondratieff. According to Dr. Kondratieff's theory, the economy consists of long waves of chaotic activity. The long waves are periods of economic change that include depressions, wars, inflation, and the like. These are demonstrated to occur approximately every fifty to sixty years.

The link between economic down cycles and the major wars is well documented. Throughout much of mankind's history, when the economy plunged into depression, one nation tried to dominate other nations—especially its neighbors—for its own economic benefit. Often during times of depression, despotic rulers rise to power with promises of a better life. When the economy does not progress the way they promise, they start a war to divert attention.

Kondratieff's observation of fifty- to sixty-year "cycles" is entirely plausible. As we can witness in our own economy, that seems to be about the time it takes for one generation to pass away and the next to repeat its mistakes. One would think that in our modern information era we could avoid the errors of our forefathers, but I assume many people in earlier generations must have thought the same thing.

> *There is sufficient data to prove that, from a historical perspective, the economy does go through periodic (and predictable) cycles.*

Enough changes are made in each successive generation so that those in charge believe they are smarter than the previous leaders. The 1929 generation had telephones, electric adding machines, even radios. I'm sure that because of those modern devices they thought they had a better handle on the economy than their predecessors did during the depression of 1893. They were completely confident that in 1929 the mistakes of the past would not be repeated.

The 1990s generation has computers with enormous information capacity; daily reports come from every corner of the globe; television keeps the American people updated (or confused); and the Federal Reserve keeps watch over the monetary system. With all these improvements, who could question our ability to avoid another economic calamity? Well, me for one. And eventually, I trust, you too.

THE CASE FOR CYCLES

There is sufficient data to prove that, from a historical perspective, the economy does go through periodic (and predictable) cycles. Approximately every fifty to sixty years since records have been kept (back to 1790), there have been major downturns lasting three years or longer. Traditionally these have been labeled major depressions. Punctuated between these major down cycles have been shorter downturns (recessions), lasting from a few months to as long as two years. A few have even lasted for as long as three years. What separated these "recessions" from the depressions was how long and how deep they were. Usually they were limited in intensity and did not endanger the stability of the overall economic system. The downturn (recession) of 1974-1976 is an example of this. Although it seemed severe to the people who lost their jobs, the recession did not threaten the overall stability of our economic system. The 1990-1991 recession fits this description also.

As the following chart shows, the cycles of the U.S. economy are not just random patterns. They appear regularly and at least somewhat predictably. The shorter recessions appear approximately every three to five years. The longer the interval between downturns, the more severe the eventual economic slump. The major downturns are just as reported—approximately every fifty to sixty years.

Cycles of Business 1812-1990

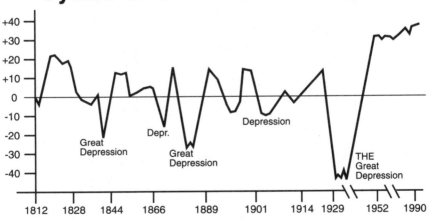

Note: Chart is designed to highlight periodic depressions.

93

A logical assumption would be to utilize this cycle record to predict economic activity in future years. And, to some extent, this can be done. Unfortunately all is not that clear. If a statistician looks long enough, he or she will find a cycle in almost everything, because basically all events are cyclical to some degree. The earth cycles the sun once a year, and the moon cycles the earth once a month. However, to presume this pattern is the same for every planetary body would yield some bad results. Each planet has its own cycle—randomly altered by the differing forces closest to it.

> *In the past decade we have dropped from the status of creditor nation to that of debtor nation.*

Similarly, each economic era has its own differing forces that shape its cycle. If we were to fill in the missing economic activities in the previous chart, you would see that there is much more activity during some periods and less during others. Cycle-theory advocates sometimes treat this conflicting data as being of little consequence but, in reality, these aberrations can lead to some bad predictions. It is my opinion that past cycles should be reviewed for major trends but not relied on for timing. In other words, by observing them we see that the economy does cycle up and down periodically. We can even tell that the cycles occur, more or less, as new generations of people forget the lessons of the past. It is also clear that each new generation brings its own unique variables. Certainly this was true when the Bolsheviks came to power in Russia, bringing Communism with them. It is also true of the United States since the New Deal established the Keynesian economic theory in our country. So the cycles are modified by the forces closest to them. But just because the economy doesn't conform to the latest cycle theory, that does not mean that we should totally ignore the problems of the past either.

CHANGES IN THE CYCLES

The period of 1987 to 1989 paralleled the 1927 to 1929 era so closely it was astounding, even alarming. Even the most ardent admirer of the Keynesian economic theory could not deny the similarities. Because of this, several best-selling books were written about "the crash of 1990."

But the economy didn't crash in 1990. Instead, we entered a relatively short-lived recession of moderate severity. As a result, many people (government economists among them) have concluded that the controls now in place are sufficient to avoid all future depressions. Such logic is both faulty and foolish.

In reality, the only conclusion that can be drawn is that we have the ability to delay the inevitable and lengthen the time between major cycles. The controls we have are adequate to alter, but not stop, the direction of our economy.

The strength of the U.S. economy is truly remarkable when some of the negatives against it are considered. For instance:

- Twenty percent of all Americans work directly for federal, state, and local governments and, as such, create no new goods and services.

- Most Americans now draw some form of government subsidy in the way of loans, grants, or direct transfer.

- Our currency is not backed by any fixed-value assets, has been inflated by huge amounts of debt, and yet is still the value standard throughout the world—at least for now.

Unfortunately, in the past decade we have dropped from the status of creditor nation to that of debtor nation. We have annual budget deficits in the hundreds of billions of dollars; we have a national debt that exceeds our government's total net worth; and the American taxpayer now works four months to pay federal taxes and a fifth month to pay state and local taxes.

Even with all our technology and material resources, we have not actually found a way to avoid the economic cycles—only delay them. If the cycle theory proves anything, it is that to delay the inevitable correction only makes the problem worse.

One of the better explanations of what happens when a normal economic cycle is broken was presented by Professor Ravi Batra in his book *The Great Depression of 1990*. Unfortunately, as the title might lead you to believe, Dr. Batra also predicted a depression in 1990. I personally believe the prediction was added more to sell books in 1989 than to pin a date on the next major depression. The information provided in the book is valid, even though the prediction wasn't.

Batra demonstrates conclusively that the U.S. economy has cycled through periods of "boom and bust" since the nation was founded, just as all other economies have. In other societies, the indicators are not as clear as they are in America, with our open society. Prior to the founding of our nation 200 years ago, most countries were governed by some form of dictatorship, as were the eastern European countries until the late 1980s. In a closed society, little information is provided about economic cycles. Also, the economy can be manipulated artificially until the whole system literally collapses. Russia, Europe, and China are classic examples of this. The evidence that the Russian leaders wanted their economy to appear stable is witnessed by the disappearance of Professor Kondratieff. Once his cycle theory was made public, showing the Russian economy also had its ups and downs, Kondratieff was sent to teach in Siberia, never to be seen or heard from again.

Prior to the collapse of communism in the Soviet Union, the people of that nation scarcely recognized the difference between the boom and bust cycles. The boom periods simply meant the government was able to spend more on the military, and the stores had two kinds of potatoes instead of just one.

Batra's information points out that the U.S. economy has experienced major down cycles approximately every thirty years. Interspersed between these major cycles were smaller cycles (recessions). The criteria he used to define a recession were a downturn of three years or less, with an unemployment rate of less than 9 percent. A depression, therefore, was defined as a downturn of more than three years, with an unemployment rate of greater than 9 percent. Certainly today we would readily agree that this would qualify as a depressed economy. If we had a downturn that lasted more than three years with 10 percent of the labor force unemployed, we would have business and personal bankruptcies on a scale never seen before in our history. In short, we are significantly more vulnerable to prolonged downturns than we were in previous generations.

Batra also points out that the severity of most of the *great* depressions (12 percent unemployment and 5 years or longer in duration) was determined primarily by whether or not a depression occurred every thirty years or every sixty years. Bear in mind that there is no mystical aspect to the cycles. They are the normal corrections for an imbalanced economy. Where the corrections are delayed because of war, excessive debt accumulation, or government manipulation, the next down cycle is more severe.

In the early sixties, no one would have believed our economy (or any other) could absorb nearly $4 trillion in debt and still survive.

If Batra's observations are correct, and I can find no objective reason why they are not, then each additional decade the correction is delayed makes the prospect of a *Great Depression* more acute.

What has clouded the issue today is that since the 1929 depression we have had unusually long periods of prosperity, interrupted by relatively minor downturns. This is Keynesian economics operating to the fullest. It is an example of the government using the controls of a central bank, depositor insurance, and debt accumulation to stimulate and support the economy during both good times and bad.

I doubt that any rational economist truly understands the total effect that such controls can have on a huge economy such as ours. When I attended economics classes in the early sixties, no one would have believed our economy (or any other) could absorb nearly $4 trillion in debt and still survive. Nor would anyone have believed that the government could manage nearly $300 billion in annual deficits. Simply put, the U.S. economy is a whole lot more resilient than anyone ever imagined, including Lord Keynes. The question is, how long can any economy survive under these conditions?

In the early 1980s I was teaching financial conferences around the country and felt compelled by the Lord to share my belief (then and now) that no economy can absorb forever the amount of debt that our economy is experiencing. But most people didn't want generalities. They wanted times and dates, so I was often asked, "How long until the economy collapses?"

At the time, I suggested the longest period I could conceive this huge transfer of wealth would continue—ten years. But more than ten years have come and gone and the economy still survives. We are deeper in debt than even the most liberal of liberals ever dreamed we would be, and yet we continue to operate in a somewhat "normal" fashion.

As you will see later, the actual deficits are almost twice as large as those admitted by the government. So why hasn't our economy collapsed? Because the American people still have confidence in "the system." The heart of the system depends on borrowing to fund the budget deficits each year. Right now the interest on a $4 trillion debt amounts to about $300 billion annually—or almost 60 percent of all personal income taxes paid. When this debt swells to $10 trillion, in nine years or so, the annual interest could total nearly $1 trillion—or more than all personal income taxes projected for that year.

Accurately predicting the precise time of a major economic downturn (great depression) is virtually impossible.

So how do we break out of this debt spiral? We don't. Unfortunately we have no choice but to continue with more of the same. It's as one of my economics professors liked to say: "He who rides on the back of a tiger cannot dismount."

The interest that most Americans are paying on their own debts should have transferred most of their wealth to the bankers and other lenders by now. The fact that a lot of it has been transferred can be seen in the large bank buildings in every city. But Uncle Sam, in the mode of Robin Hood, has been taking some of the earnings from the rich and giving it back to the poor by way of transfer payments. The transfer payments are not enough to keep them from being poor, but the payments are enough to allow them to continue participating in the economy. Slowly but surely, however, the middle class is being eliminated. The "poor" get federal subsidies for education, housing, health care, even food. The wealthy have enough to provide these benefits for themselves. The middle class borrow against the little equity they have remaining to pay for what they need.

We have another "catch 22" in the transfer of wealth out of our country. As the national debt continues to grow, our dependence on foreign loans will continue to mount.

A short-range solution will be more taxes. One recurring suggestion is to tax the "wealthy" more. The difficulty is that even if the tax burden was doubled on everyone making over $200,000 a year, that money would operate our government for only 28 days! Also, stripping the wealthy of all their surpluses is a little like killing the goose that lays the golden eggs. The poor don't invest for the future. They need all they have just to live.

The second part of this catch 22 is the danger of foreign investors not lending us the money we need. If they stop lending, then we must print the money (monetize the debt). When we begin this process, hyperinflation is certain to follow. So what do we do? It's a little like a cowboy in the old west riding his horse to death trying to avoid the Indians chasing him. He knows if he keeps on riding, his horse will eventually collapse. But he also knows if he stops, *he* will die. So he rides on, hoping for a miracle.

I have concluded that accurately predicting the precise time of a major economic downturn (great depression) is virtually impossible. Furthermore, until we get inside the "window of statistical probability," all attempts to establish a time is purely guesswork. The window of statistical probability occurs when the circumstances get so bad economically that no amount of further manipulation is possible to keep the economy going at a reasonably normal pace.

Let's assume this "window," where we can accurately determine what is going to happen in the economy, is one year. In other words, only when we get within one year of a major economic collapse will the indicators be clear. What we need to do is establish a template of these economic indicators (I will label them "cracks") and continue sliding it along the time line until the indicators line up. Then we will have an indication of the actual timing. It is much like making a template of a small section of a road map. You slide the template along the map until it matches a section on the full map. Then you can see where you are in the bigger picture.

One difficulty with our economic "template" is that, at best, it can provide only one year or less of warning. A second is, if the indicators are wrong, we may miss the "window" entirely.

I am not totally convinced that all the economic indicators signaling a depression are clear enough to make such a template. However, I do believe there are sufficient indicators available to give at least some warning. It is entirely possible that the economy has been manipulated by our government so long that an accurate long-term projection is not possible today. That's why so many of the cycle theorists have been wrong thus far. But these cycles can provide a reasonably accurate picture of what happened just prior to the great depressions of the past. Many of the same indicators should be present prior to the next one.

I have a friend in the commodities business who developed a computer model of most of the past cycles in the commodities market. Each of these cycles had slightly different but predictable patterns that occurred prior to a major upturn or downturn in the market. It seemed reasonable to assume that if he programmed all these factors into a computer and checked them daily he would be able to predict future trends in the commodities market.

Since there are tens of thousands of daily variables that can affect the price of commodities, it is impossible for humans to do this. But with the high-speed processing capabilities of modern computers, it is a simple task to check a million different variables every second if necessary. So my friend programmed all of the past data into his computer and then applied this very sophisticated program to the real commodities market. The result: It didn't work.

This perplexed him because when he applied the program to past events it worked perfectly. In other words, if he took all the data available prior to a known (major) market downturn and verified it against the data just *prior* to the event, his program signaled a warning. His quandary was, if it would work looking backward, why wouldn't it work looking forward?

Measuring from the end of the last great depression would place the next major depression in the year 2000.

The fact is, today the commodities market is subject to different factors than those seen in the past. For instance, the program failed to predict a major drop in soybean prices during the Falkland Islands war between Argentina and England. Why? Because there had never been such a war before. Common sense said that soybean prices should have gone up since Argentina was a large exporter of soybeans at the time. Indeed, that is exactly what the program predicted, but since England overwhelmed Argentina in the brief skirmish, the market reacted favorably and soybean prices dropped.

So my friend went back to his computer and began to program some "what if" variables. He also realized the program would not be able to look very far into the future, because the variables became impossibly complicated. He asked the program to predict only the immediate reaction the market might take to circumstances around it; basically he built a "template."

The result is that he now has a program with an accuracy of 70 percent on short-range market reactions. Seventy percent may not sound all that great to a noncommodities dealer, but in the commodities business it is phenomenal.

The greatest discovery he made is that the program is over 90 percent accurate in predicting major market downturns. In the commodities business, it is more critical to avoid major downturns than to hit major upturns because the losses in one bad market can wipe out years of profits.

In the case of the economy, the same basic principle holds true: Avoiding one major depression is more important than profiting in ten growth periods.

THE SIXTY-YEAR CYCLES

From all the statistical data now available, I am convinced that the normal period between major down cycles (depressions) is in the sixty-year range. This is not an absolute by any means, and plus or minus 10 percent is six years, so flexibility is essential.

I also believe that the sixty-year period should be measured from the end of one major depression to the beginning of the next. Measuring from the end of the last great depression would place the next major depression in the year 2000 (plus or minus the variable). Only time will tell whether this is the correct timing or not. But if we can develop the sliding indicators (template), perhaps the next depression can be detected before it happens.

8
THE GROWTH
OF DEBT

Kenneth was from a long line of farmers. He inherited nearly 1,000 acres in the midwest from his father. It was in the heart of America's grain belt, and the black gold, spoken of by the Dutch and Irish immigrants who cut the forests, was the soil.

Until he went to college, Kenneth had risen every day at 5:30 A.M. to help with the chores. On a large farm like theirs, most of the manual labor was to keep the machinery going, but Kenneth's father was from the old school and believed a farm boy needed to know the soil so Kenneth always had a five-acre tract of his own to farm. He used the old '46 Ford tractor—still in use after thirty years. Kenneth loved the farm and had only one desire in life: to become a farmer like his father before him.

Kenneth's father realized that the operation of a large farm required a lot more information than in previous generations, so he sent Kenneth off to the state agricultural college where he learned the latest planting techniques, scientific animal husbandry, how to utilize computers, and, most important, agrarian economics.

"Today's modern farmer learns how to use his assets wisely," the professors told their students. "Equity is idle capital and is as wasteful to farming as weak seed."

The school offered courses in how to use the latest government farm support programs to get better yield (monetarily) from the modern farm. Kenneth learned that the federal government would not only lend farmers money at subsidized interest rates, but would actually pay them not to grow certain crops. By rotating the land into the soil bank program, a farmer could revitalize the soil while getting paid by the government to do so.

"The day of the independent farmer is over," Kenneth heard over and over again. Adapt or fail—that was the byword in modern agricultural schools.

Kenneth graduated from college and worked with his father for nearly ten years, during which time he attempted with no success to get his father to apply for the farm subsidy program.

His father's response was, "I have never taken welfare, and I don't intend to start now. You never get something for nothing," he cautioned Kenneth. "One day you'll run the farm, and you would do well to remember that."

Unfortunately, "Common Sense 101" was not a required course in college, and Kenneth was chafing at the bit to apply what he had been taught. He respected his father but felt he was too old-fashioned. Fresh in his mind was the message his professors had implanted: "adapt or fail."

Eventually Kenneth could not stand to wait any longer. He told his father that he wanted to start a farm of his own and prove what he could do by using modern methodology. Kenneth's father, nearly 70, decided that it was time to retire and turned the operation over to him.

Kenneth immediately applied to the soil bank program and committed nearly three hundred acres to the government's "don't grow food" program so generously provided by the American taxpayers. In return he received a subsidy of nearly $50,000 a year not to grow something he wasn't planning to grow anyway.

Using the crop subsidy, he then applied to the Farm Loan Administration for money to expand his operation. With the subsequent loans he modernized his equipment, and he used the tax credits to shelter virtually all the income from the farm bank subsidy. With virtually no effort he increased the farm's income by $50,000 a year, tax free (less the interest on the loan of course). The farm loan was a 4 percent expense, of which approximately half was returned in taxes. So he netted a 2 percent loan. Not a bad deal by any standard.

Kenneth was a microcosm of the Keynesian economic theory: The government can decide best how the country's resources should be used.

As other farms became available, Kenneth made additional loans against the increasing equity in his farm to purchase them. Although the debt continued to grow, the equity in the land grew even faster. Bankers were anxious to grant Kenneth any loans he wanted; he was the showcase of the Federal Farm Loan credit system.

Twice in the next five years Kenneth was named "Farmer of the Year" by national magazines. He was known as an astute young farmer who epitomized the best the "system" had to offer. Even Kenneth's father had to admit that the farm was running better and making more profit than ever before. What he didn't know, of course, was that the debt was over $2 million by the end of the fifth year. Prospects were great, and the government was planning bigger and better subsidy programs at the behest of the politicians from the farm belt.

Kenneth's farm covered more than 10,000 acres and, other than a few small tracts that had not yet become available, was virtually contiguous, making his farm the largest in the district. At age 35, Kenneth was well on his way to becoming the wealthiest farmer in his entire state. He knew all the politicians by name, and they often used him as their feature attraction when asking for more subsidies from Washington. Kenneth was a microcosm of the Keynesian economic theory: The *government* can decide best how the country's resources should be used.

Then suddenly inflation struck, and loans that had been running at 8 percent escalated to 12 and, later, to 20 percent. The low-interest loans Kenneth had originally received had been supplanted by variable-rate, high-interest loans to a large degree.

But the added costs didn't particularly worry Kenneth. Even at the higher interest rates, he had the cash flow to survive until the economy turned around again. Besides, he knew he could always sell a part of the farm, if absolutely necessary. The federal subsidies had made his land very valuable.

What Kenneth didn't know was that the federal government was having trouble with its own budget, and one of the areas to be reduced was farm subsidies. When Ronald Reagan came into office, he brought with him some temporary, but very harsh, controls on federal spending. Within a few months, the mood in Washington had shifted from praising the farmers who fell into line with the subsidy program to accusing them of being greedy money grubbers who were getting rich at the expense of the poor.

The private sector debt is growing just as wildly as the public sector debt.

Suddenly Kenneth found himself on the outside looking in, as far as Washington was concerned. The farm subsidy program was altered to prohibit many of the big farms from participating. Congressional investigations were discussed to see which politicians had benefited by endorsing the big farmers.

Without warning, farm land plummeted in value as buyers realized the free ride was coming to an end. Kenneth's bankers began demanding that he reduce some of his debt. To do so required that he put a portion of his land up for sale. As soon as that word got out, land prices in his area plummeted even further.

The bankers, now concerned about Kenneth's solvency, demanded payment in full. When he couldn't comply, they forced a liquidation. In less than six years, Kenneth had gone from inheriting a thousand-acre, debt-free farm to being wiped out.

When the final parcel of land was auctioned off, Kenneth had lost a three-generation farm, all the equipment, his parents' home, and was left owing nearly $2 million to the Farm Credit Association and several banks.

It's interesting to note that the land wasn't changed, and people still needed food. But Kenneth no longer could operate any portion of the farm profitably. He didn't just lose what he had increased; he lost everything! Proverbs 23:4-5 speaks to this principle when it says, *"Do not weary yourself to gain riches, cease from your consideration of it. When you set your eyes on it, it is gone. For wealth certainly makes itself wings, like an eagle that flies toward the heavens."*

THE ERROR

At first glance anyone with common sense would say, "He overextended, and he should have known better." If that's true (and it is), what about the rest of the country? Kenneth was not doing anything the majority of American businesspeople are not doing right this minute. The private sector debt is growing just as wildly as the public sector debt. The only difference is that the government's debt is published for all to see. The private sector's debt is spread out over thousands of individuals and businesses, so it looks less imposing.

The debt picture in America today is alarming. Not only is the size unmanageable but, as noted previously, much of the interest paid is leaving the country. The small debtors borrow from the banks (and others). The banks place a large portion of their earnings in government securities (otherwise known as debt). The government in turn pays out a huge chunk of this in interest to foreign lenders, who then use their profits to reinvest in American businesses. A whole nation is literally selling its birthright, as Esau did for the proverbial "bowl of soup."

A look at America's debt structure today should be enough to get the attention of any doubters.

PERSONAL DEBT

Prior to the 1920s, Americans were characterized as frugal, self-reliant people who had a strong faith in God. Debt was certainly not unknown, but it would have been unusual for the average American to borrow for anything other than the purchase of a home, and even that loan was for no more than seven years or less.

It is not by chance that most private debt was limited to a payout of seven years or less. The plan for all lending had been adopted from the Bible and, as such, the duration of loans was patterned after the year of remission described in Deuteronomy 15:1-2: *"At the end of every seven years you shall grant a remission of debts. And this is the manner of remission: every creditor shall release what he has loaned to his neighbor; he shall not exact it of his neighbor and his brother, because the Lord's remission has been proclaimed."*

As I said earlier, the real trend in consumer debt began after World War II, with the return of millions of GIs needing homes, cars, and jobs. Americans had a great deal of disposable income and were able to handle debt on long-term purchases such as homes. A look at the average family's disposable income in 1960 gives a clear picture of where the country was financially.

By the early seventies the great credit card binge was under way.

The average income was approximately $6,700 per year. Out of that income, the average family paid 8 percent in direct taxes (including Social Security). Their home costs amounted to 22 percent of net income. The average home sold for just over $8,000, was about 1,000 square feet, carried a 21-year loan at 4.5 percent, and was soon to yield some huge appreciation.

A new car in 1960 sold for approximately $2,100 and could be financed for as long as 18 months, provided the buyer put down at least 25 percent.

Beyond that, the average family carried no debt except, occasionally, some credit for appliances financed by one of the national retailers such as Sears or J.C. Penney.

It was actually this seemingly insignificant area of retail credit that would spark the consumer credit binge in America. By the mid-sixties, most of the major retailers were offering credit for purchases. Surprisingly, consumers accepted the idea of retail credit, even though the interest rates were significantly higher than that of commercial lenders, like banks. The key factor was that the retailers made credit available to many families (especially young couples) who could not qualify for bank loans.

In the forties, fifties, and early sixties, bankers were noted for their conservative approach to lending. Basically, they wouldn't lend for consumables and wouldn't lend to people who should not have had credit. In other words, you had to earn the right to receive credit.

I can recall applying for my first home loan in 1962, while working at Cape Canaveral in Florida. Although I had a good job and could well afford the payments of $86 per month on a 3-bedroom home that sold for $8,200 (wouldn't we like to see that again?), because I had no credit history, the bank turned me down. Only later, after we had saved an additional $1,000, were we able to qualify for a loan.

Credit cards were a rarity at that time, with the exception of specialty cards such as American Express. In 1963 I applied for a credit card (although I didn't particularly need it), but I was turned down because American Express required at least a $10,000 per year income to qualify for one of their cards.

I'm sure you get the picture: Americans had adjusted to home mortgages, car loans, and some consumer financing for major appliances, but the credit boom was still to come.

By the mid-sixties financial reports from the big retailers began to reflect huge profits from the consumer credit they were issuing. Suddenly the rush was on to tap into that lucrative market. Stores like Sears were making as much on financing as they were making on the merchandise, and with a whole lot less effort. Remarkably the defaults by consumers had proved to be nominal by banking standards. Americans were prone to protect their reputations and pay their bills. By the early seventies the great credit card binge was under way.

In the housing area more and more home buyers entered the market created by long-term mortgages. Soon the law of supply and demand began to kick in. The law (rule really) of supply and demand is simple: With an abundant supply of any product and a shortage of available buyers, prices will remain constant or fall; with a shortage of any product and an abundance of buyers, prices will rise.

In this case, the availability of long-term financing for housing opened up the product (homes) to many additional buyers. Consequently they bid the price of homes up, and the housing boom was under way.

As prices escalated, the number of home buyers who could qualify began to decline. Faced with a declining demand, the lending institutions simply lengthened the terms of the mortgages, thus qualifying more buyers. This spiral took the average mortgage period from twelve years to thirty years in just one decade. At the same time, the average home escalated in price from $8,600 to $26,000.

This sparked a real estate boom that was to continue for the next twenty-five years. Americans began to view their homes not only as dwelling places but also as good investments.

Any supply and demand spiral can grow only until the price of the product (homes in this case) is beyond what the average consumer can afford, even with the long-term financing. Then prices will begin to fall again. The reason this process was delayed in the case of residential housing was not just long-term financing but also because potential buyers took on dual incomes (husband and wife) to qualify; they stretched their housing budget from 22 percent in 1960 to more than 40 percent in 1990 and took on some "creative" mortgages to expand their buying range.

The most recent "creative" mortgage plan is the adoption of a 90-year payment schedule. Effectively, Americans have mortgaged their futures to buy the home they have come to expect. Even the recent trend back to smaller, simpler homes has not brought the average home within the income range of the average family. The current median income per family is about $40,000. Based on this income, the median price of a home should be approximately

$80,000. Instead, it sells for slightly less than $142,000. Those who buy at these prices, and many do, find themselves in constant financial difficulties.

One problem with so much consumer indebtedness is that the average wage earner is also the government's primary provider.

Since the 1986 Tax Reform Act, which allows deductions only for home-related loans, home equity debt has grown at an alarming rate. According to the American Bankers Association, home equity debt increased by 120 percent between 1985 and 1991. Home equity "lines of credit" were up 475 percent. As Americans borrowed against the equity in their homes, they used a larger portion of their disposable incomes.

American banks now hold more than $3 trillion in first mortgages as collateral for what are considered the most stable loans in their portfolios. In addition, they hold nearly $500 billion in home equity loans and credit lines above the first mortgages. These also are considered some of the "best" loans. Clearly, many American homeowners have transferred the wealth stored in their homes to the lenders. In this case, it leaves both in jeopardy. Given the wrong set of economic circumstances, the homeowners will default, leaving the banks with huge inventories of homes they can't sell.

CONSUMER DEBT

The rise in consumer debt over the last 20 years has been nothing less than phenomenal—from approximately $132 billion in 1970 to more than $777 billion in 1991! And the alarming fact about consumer debt is that it is available to virtually anyone and usually carries an annual finance charge of 18 percent and higher.

Literally, Americans are working for the "company store" again. They labor at their jobs to pay the usurious interest they have come to accept as "normal." The increase in personal bankruptcies has grown at an alarming pace. In 1970 the total of personal bankruptcies was under 100,000. In 1980 it was 259,160; but by 1985 bankruptcies had risen to 312,000. In 1990 there were 685,439 and, by 1993, the number was 897,231. This is not a problem. It is a symptom of a society awash in "easy money," which is what credit seems to be today. Eventually the majority of households will reach the stage where they cannot repay what they owe; nor will they be able to borrow more. At that point, the economy must stop while the debt is either repudiated (by a depression), devalued (by hyperinflation), or repaid (unthinkable).

A CATCH 22

One problem with so much consumer indebtedness is that the average wage earner is also the government's primary provider. As I said previously, in spite of all the rhetoric you hear from the liberal side of the media and from the Congress, it is not the wealthy who can carry the tax burden in America (or any other country). The truth is, there just simply are not enough of them.

At this point, I would like to stop and offer an observation that is critical to our economy's long-term survival.

The system of economics by which our wealth was developed is called "capitalism." Capitalism means that private individuals with a surplus of capital are willing to risk it to make more capital. That process inevitably makes some of them wealthy. But also in the process others are employed, and some of them save enough to invest and become "Capitalists."

There is nothing inherently bad or evil about this system, as the media often represent. It is this capitalistic system that has allowed us the ability to support other poorer countries, defend our freedoms, and do away with child labor.

If we now treat all the wealthy "Capitalists" like criminals simply because some are criminals, we will lose our economic base and we will sink to the level of "socialist" countries such as Russia, China, Yugoslavia, Poland, Hungary, and so on.

The Bible does not teach against the accumulation of wealth as some apparently believe. It teaches against greed, ego, and a disregard for the needs of others. Anyone who thinks that the lack of wealth is a cure for these sins has only to visit any major inner city in America today.

The vast majority of people with a surplus of money did not steal it or cheat someone else to get it. They made it doing what they are best at. Anyone who now believes the government can do a better job of managing that money by stripping it from those who have it needs to look at the evidence to the contrary. The government does not invest; it consumes. Politicians who use the system to their advantage would be quite willing to consume the nation's "seed corn" if it would help them get re-elected. Our single hope of economic recovery (outside of divine intervention) resides in the American entrepreneur's ability to see a need and fill it. Without the available capital, that is not possible. I am not touting the wealthy because I am wealthy, because I am not; but I do know that America must have investment capital to survive, and the poor just don't have it.

Borrowed capital became the primary means of starting new businesses in the late sixties and seventies.

It is the average income wage earner to whom the government will always turn when there is a need for more tax money. The quickest and least painful way (for the politicians) to raise money to keep the government operating is to create some new "revenue enhancements." Since tax increases are politically unpopular, the common method used is to initiate a tax bill designed to "soak the rich" and drop in a few revenue enhancers, such as eliminating the interest deduction for mortgages or the write-offs for contributions. There are several other possibilities, but these two will generate nearly $100 billion a year in new taxes by themselves. The unfortunate by-product of this action is to reduce the average consumer's level of spending. Therein lies the catch 22.

The increased tax revenues are offset by decreased spending. The decreased spending means fewer sales, which means fewer jobs, which means less revenue. . . .

BUSINESS DEBT

The trend in business debt is not as startling as that of the consumers, but it is equally as disastrous. As of 1990, American corporations were paying out 7.7 percent of their gross incomes in interest alone—compared to 3.8 percent in 1970. Much of this is debt on nonproductive capital, such as the junk bonds used for leveraged buy-outs during the eighties. Other companies that were not engaged in leveraged buy-outs took on considerable debt during this time in an effort to make their businesses less enticing to a buy-out. These were the so-called poison pills swallowed by so many companies.

A look at American business prior to the sixties shows that the majority of businesses were started and expanded by selling equity. Basically this meant selling stock in the company and giving up a portion of the equity. Two things happened in the sixties and seventies that changed the funding strategies of most businesses from equity to debt.

First, credit became readily available at competitive rates. In fact, the cost of renting the money was considerably less than the profits that could be made by using the money in the business. There is no question that it made economic sense to borrow money at 6 percent and invest it in a business that could yield 10 to 12 percent a year on the money. Borrowed capital became the primary means of starting new businesses in the late sixties and seventies. As business loans became more commonplace, companies even shifted to debt funding for expansion as well as for acquisition. By the mid-seventies debt was the acceptable means of starting and operating a business.

The second change was that the cost of issuing stock became prohibitively expensive for many small companies. The complexities of the securities laws and the risks in the stock market forced most start-up operations to rely totally on debt funding.

Limited partnerships were an attempt by the securities groups to provide an alternative means of selling equity. Unfortunately the abuses by fast-talking promoters virtually killed this avenue for equity funding in the eighties. Eventually the abuse of tax laws in limited partnerships caused the demise of that system.

The vast majority of equity in American companies is still found in stocks traded on the two major exchanges. But the largest portions of these stocks are sold investor to investor. Their sales do not particularly help the parent company, except to the extent that stockholders' equity goes up. For a company to profit from the sale of its stock there must be either a new issue offered for sale or existing treasury stock sold. Most transactions do virtually nothing to benefit the company's daily operations except that it makes loans easier to acquire, based on equity values.

The debt burden of most businesses in America today is so great that virtually any slowdown in economic activity can place them in jeopardy. This was clearly demonstrated in the early stages of the 1990 recession when several major department store chains filed for bankruptcy reorganization after a poor selling season. These retailers had taken on so much debt that even a single slow season wiped them out. Some were chains that had been in operation for five decades or more, like the Federated Department Stores.

Certainly competition from mass marketers, such as Wal-Mart and Kmart, had affected these retailers to some extent. But generally they were not direct competitors in the same market share. It was excessive debt that did them in; and it is excessive debt that will do in a great many more businesses in any prolonged downturn. Unfortunately this presents a dilemma to the politicians in a government-controlled economy like ours: How can we collect all the taxes possible without killing off the businesses that employ the people who pay the taxes? I believe the answer to that question is the key to the coming economic earthquake. . . .

9

GOVERNMENT DEBT

Imagine this scenario if you will: A family of four making $3,000 a month is spending $4,000 a month and has been doing so for more than five years. Their total assets consist of a home and two cars—all mortgaged for more than their resale value. Their total debt to date is $150,000 in unsecured liabilities, plus an additional $100,000 they have borrowed from their retirement account, which must be repaid with interest in the next twenty years. And one last item: They borrowed their parents' life savings to help pay the interest on their debt and now are obligated to support them, in addition to their own current spending.

Let's assume this couple has come to you for advice about what they should do at this point. How would you counsel them?

Having counseled many couples in the past, I can tell you the options:

1. They can try to generate more income, but essentially this husband is working at his capacity, so the most he can hope to

get is a part-time job that will generate another couple of hundred a month.

2. They can file for bankruptcy protection and just not pay most of their creditors. Of course this will destroy their reputation and their credit rating for the indefinite future. In addition, it won't help the repayment of their retirement account or the money they have borrowed from their parents.

3. They can find someone who will lend them the money to consolidate all their debts. But, since the total debt is still beyond their ability to pay even if they consolidate, they will need enough extra to make the monthly payments for the next several years, at which time they are hoping that something miraculous will happen to pay off the entire debt.

Actually, now you find out that they have not come to you for advice but for a consolidation loan, since you seem to be doing pretty well yourself.

The government has an income of approximately $1.2 trillion a year. It is spending approximately $1.5 trillion a year.

Logically, I hope you would say, "It seems to me that you need to get realistic and face the facts: You simply spend too much for your income. Sell whatever you can, pay down the debt, cut back your spending, and start paying back what you owe. More money won't help at this point."

Good advice, I would say. Only the couple in this case is our government. The numbers used are smaller than the government's total income and debt, but the ratios are correct.

The government has an income of approximately $1.2 trillion a year. It is spending approximately $1.5 trillion a year.

The gross "on-budget" debt of the government is $4.3 trillion as of 1993; the "off-budget" debt, which includes unfunded retirement liabilities, is estimated to be $6 trillion more.

The money the government has borrowed from its "parents" is the Social Security Trust Funds taken from millions of honest Americans who believe they are contributing to their own retirement accounts.

We are in a mess that is getting messier every day, and there appears to be no interest in trying to resolve the problems. The only concern shown by most politicians is how to fund the deficits without changing the system or their own spending habits, which include incomes four times higher than the average workers they represent and a very generous retirement plan.

HOW IMPORTANT IS THE DEBT?

In the last several years a new theory has been developed in Washington that the national debt really doesn't matter since it is a smaller ratio of the country's gross domestic product (GDP) than it was thirty years ago. That is not true.

In 1980 the GDP was $2.64 trillion and the total debt was $908 billion—a ratio of 3.44 to 1. In 1992 the GDP was $6.3 trillion and the total debt was $4.3 trillion—a ratio of 1.47 to 1. Add to that figure the unfunded liabilities and you get a better picture of the total. With a real national debt (current debt plus future liabilities) in excess of $10 trillion, the total debt is actually greater than the GDP. But even if it were not, the argument still makes no sense. The very fact that so much debt has been used in the economy inflates the GDP. For example: If housing contributes $1 trillion to the GDP, how much of that is inflation, created by excessive long-term financing?

To determine this, just assume that today a law was passed making all mortgages illegal so that no home could be sold with a mortgage. Therefore, if you wanted to sell your home, you would have to find a cash buyer.

Under these circumstances what would a $100,000 home (present value) sell for across the country? Not $100,000—that's for sure. On a cash-only basis, it would probably sell for about $20,000 (the supply and demand rule). We can logically assume that everything above that amount has been added through debt-funded inflation. The national debt has added to the GDP by virtue of inflation.

But let's use this argument: Sure, the GDP is calculated in inflated dollars, but so is the debt itself. The next issue: How much of the government's income does it take to make the payments now, as compared to even 12 years ago?

In 1982 it took approximately 19 percent of the government's income to service its gross debt. To date, it requires approximately 25 percent (57 percent of all personal income taxes). I would like someone to explain how the national debt doesn't really matter today!

FIGURES DON'T LIE

As the old cliché goes: "Figures don't lie, but liars can figure." The following chart clearly shows the ever-widening gap between federal revenues and federal spending.

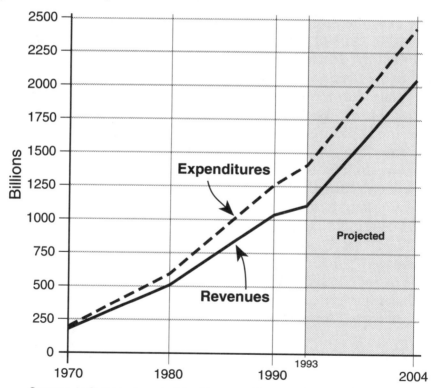

Expenditures vs. Revenues

Source: U.S. Department of the Treasury, Congressional Budget Office

Because of the growing debt problem, a new law was passed in 1985 requiring the government not only to live within its income but also to balance the federal budget in six years and begin repaying some of the existing debt. This law, the Gramm-Rudman Act, was to be the guiding force behind fiscal responsibilities.

When the budget and national debt began to swell in the seventies, some conservative taxpayers began a "balance the budget" movement to require the government to live within its means. There was even talk of a constitutional amendment to force a balanced budget on the politicians, since they didn't seem willing to do so voluntarily.

When Ronald Reagan came into the presidency, some members of Congress began to feel the momentum building toward such an amendment. There was even talk of opening another constitutional convention to correct some other liberal interpretations of the constitution. Suddenly the Congress was open to a new law requiring a balanced budget. Thus, they approved the Gramm-Rudman Act—first in 1985, and when that didn't work, they tried again in 1987. The Gramm-Rudman laws set down specific yearly guidelines for reducing the budget deficits according to the following chart.

Deficit Growth Under Gramm-Rudman Acts

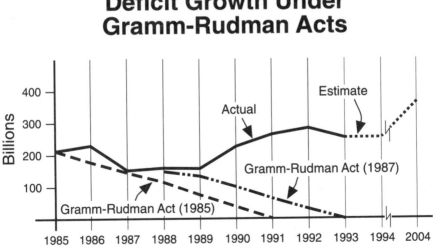

Source: Congressional Quarterly, U.S. Department of the Treasury, and Congressional Budget Office

121

As you can see, the original law required that the federal budget be balanced by the year 1991. In addition, overruns in excess of the prescribed amounts initiated automatic spending cuts. Unfortunately, both laws left some "loop-holes" and depended too much on the *integrity* of those in charge of our government—something that is sorely missing today. As you can see from the comparison, the legal annual deficit and the actual deficits grew further apart each year.

The Congress and the president simply found "creative" ways around the law. One method was to siphon the funds out of the Social Security Trust account and use them to help reduce the deficits. As I said previously, since the theft is considered an internal transfer of assets, it is not reflected as a debt (very creative, huh?).

Another technique was to transfer budget overruns into the next fiscal year. You might logically think that would create an even greater problem the next year. Not so! All you have to do is transfer that amount (and more) into the next year (now that's also very creative).

The third method was even more creative. Since the budget and its deficits are calculated on projected income, it is a simple process to calculate more income than is realistic during the budget process. Then when the overruns are greater than anticipated, the budget managers simply say, "Oops," and ask for a special dispensation for that error.

Another creative technique used in the budgeting process was simply to ignore the law altogether by shifting more spending "off budget." If you or I did that, it would be punishable by fines and imprisonment; but for our elected "leaders," it is "business as usual." In the adoption of the "balanced budget" law, the Congress excluded the majority of spending from the budget process. Thus, areas such as welfare, Medicare, Social Security, federal retirement, and the like were exempted from the mandatory reductions. To balance the budget based on actual income and expenses would require the virtual elimination of other "flexible" areas of spending, such as defense. The exclusions made a balanced budget virtually impossible.

I'm sure you get the picture by now. The net effect was to continue the budget overruns irrespective of the law. Then, in 1990, Congress and the White House agreed to suspend the Gramm-Rudman deficit targets for three years. Upon taking office, President Clinton suspended the targets for a while longer. After all, the elected leaders of our nation exempt themselves from every other law they require of the voters. Why not exempt themselves from the laws passed to control their actions?

RUNAWAY DEBT

When the Grace Commission was authorized by President Reagan in 1983, it was a privately funded, nonpartisan group, directed to find ways to cut government waste, which they did. But as a by-product, they began to look into the huge budget deficits and resultant debt being accumulated by the government. As Harry Figgie, a member of the commission, said, "It wasn't just alarming. It was frightening."

At the time of the Commission's report in 1984, they estimated the total federal debt might reach $3 trillion by the year 2000. As we saw earlier, it exceeded that level in 1991.

Every time the taxpayers give the Congress $1.00 extra, it spends $1.68.

Lower interest rates helped to lower long-term debt projections but, even so, all realistic estimates now place the on-budget gross debt at $8 to $10 trillion by the year 2004. That may sound distant to those of us who have lived most of our lives in the twentieth century, but it is only ten years away.

The following chart demonstrates what the accumulated deficit will look like in just a few years. I included this chart because it is critical to understand that the debt is going to destroy our economy if it is not brought under control quickly.

Growth of the Federal Debt

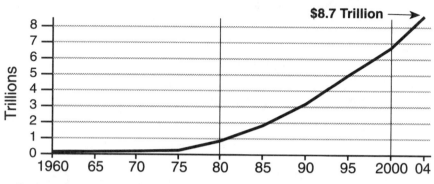

Source: Department of the Treasury, Congressional Budget Office
Note: Projections after 1999 are extrapolated from CBO data.

Mr. Figgie relates a story that typifies what happens in the budgeting process in Washington. He said that in 1986 the Congress adopted $152 billion of the $424 billion in savings identified by the Grace Commission. At the same time, because of the urgent concern about the skyrocketing debt, the Congress voted for a $50 billion tax increase (the 1986 Tax "Reform" Act).

As a result of these two changes, which amounted to a $38 billion decrease in spending for five consecutive years and a $50 billion increase in revenues, the annual deficit, which was $128 billion at that time, should have been $40 billion by 1991 ($128 minus $38 = $90 minus $50 = $40). Instead, the "on-budget" annual deficit hit $269.5 billion. That did not include the S&L deficits, which were considered "off budget."

As Mr. Figgie points out, every time the taxpayers give the Congress $1.00 extra, it spends $1.68.

This discussion about the federal debt is an attempt to bring you up to date on what's *really* happening with the deficit in Washington. Not only is it out of control, there appear to be few rational voices in the Capitol trying to straighten out the mess. I can't emphasize too strongly that the federal debt (as well as the private sector debt) can and will destroy our economy. Americans who have worked hard all their lives will see their life savings consumed by runaway inflation. Remember that the politicians who tell you that the debt is irrelevant are the same ones who said the following: More money will eliminate poverty; taxes will never be more than 2 percent; pornography is a personal issue; and sex education will solve teen pregnancies. With that kind of a track record, I doubt that their insight about this issue is any better.

The one thing you can be sure of is that when the deficits begin to go ballistic and rob businesses of the capital they need to operate, and when huge chunks of American industry are sold off to foreign investors to secure needed operating capital, the Congress will hold investigations to determine why this was allowed to happen.

At the current rate of growth, the federal deficits will feed approximately $6 trillion dollars of additional debt into the economy between now and the year 2004. There never has been anything approaching this level of debt funding in the history of mankind in so short a period of time, even on a percentage basis. The effects of this will be felt throughout the U.S. and ultimately the world's economies. It is estimated that, at most, approximately $3 to $5 trillion is available from all sources to fund this deficit. That leaves only two logical conclusions: Either the government will take the necessary steps to control the budget and reduce the deficits drastically, or they will resort to monetizing the debt by printing massive amounts of new currency.

I don't know what your analysis is but, based on observation, I find it hard to believe our government leaders have either the inclination or the will to cut their spending sufficiently.

Does anyone realistically believe that politicians are going to make the kinds of choices necessary to balance the budget?

Not counting offsetting surpluses from Social Security and other "trust fund" accounts, the Congressional Budget Office estimates that the government will overspend by nearly $2 trillion between now and 1999.

Allow me to outline what kinds of cuts would be necessary to bring the budget into balance over five years. This does not deal with reducing the national debt—only the annual deficits that are adding to it presently.

1. Federal payrolls would need to be reduced by approximately 40 percent. This would require the dismissal of more than a million employees, saving approximately $40 billion annually.

2. Means-tested welfare programs would need to be reduced by 25 percent, saving perhaps $50 billion annually.

3. Defense spending, which is already being cut, would need to be reduced by another 25 percent, saving $70 billion annually. (This would require the closure of obsolete military installations all across the country, resulting in the additional loss of hundreds of thousands of jobs in civilian-related businesses.) It would also necessitate recalling many of our U.S. military personnel stationed outside the United States.

4. Programs, such as student loans, farm supports-education grants, and the myriad of other government-subsidized programs would need to be cut across the board by at least 50 percent, saving about $20 billion a year.

As you can see, even with these cuts the budget has been reduced by only $180 billion a year. We would need to make another round of cuts to trim out the additional $180 billion in actual overspending, if the government could not shift any spending to the off-budget category.

My obvious question is: Does anyone realistically believe that politicians are going to make the kinds of choices necessary to balance the budget? And would the average American be willing to make the sacrifices necessary to allow such cuts, even if the politicians wanted to do so?

Unfortunately this is not the end of the debt spiral; it is barely the beginning unless an immediate attitude adjustment is made in our country. There are some future trends that can make the present level of spending look like the "good ol' days."

We have some pending problems that need resolution, and unfortunately the common attitude is that throwing money at problems will make them go away. One might think we should know better, based on our "success" record to date.

Logic and common sense seem to play small parts in our present society, as confirmed by the following facts:

- We get soft on prosecuting criminals and then wonder why crime increases.

- We legalize abortion and then wonder why there are fewer kids to fill the schools.

- We protect child pornography as free speech and then wonder why so many kids are abducted and murdered.

- We take discipline out of the classrooms and wonder why kids don't learn as well.

- We entice young couples to get into debt and then wonder why the divorce rate is so high.

The list could go on and on. The answer is found in God's Word. All of these things are but *symptoms*. The real problem is that we have removed God from the decision-making process in America today. When any nation does this, evil will prosper. This is not the fault of the politicians; they are responding to the wishes of the most vocal groups. It is that the unprincipled people around us seem to be more committed to their agenda than the true "moral majority" is to theirs. This conforms with what the Lord said in Luke 16:8: *"And his master praised the unrighteous steward because he had acted shrewdly; for the sons of this age are more shrewd in relation to their own kind than the sons of light."*

What I have tried to do thus far is bring you up-to-date on what has happened in the economy. Even if we could freeze the spending right where it is, the debt still would eventually become unmanageable, simply because of the accumulating interest. The following graph shows the annual interest "payments" just since 1980. Interest "payments" is a misnomer. The interest is not actually being paid. It is being borrowed and added to the debt. So, in reality, we are paying interest on the interest from previous years.

Interest on the Public Debt

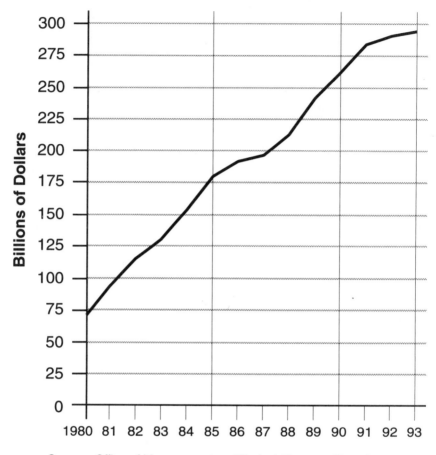

Source: Office of Management and Budget, Treasury Department

As the graph on the next page shows, projected interest on the national debt will continue a steep and steady climb for the foreseeable future. Two things are likely to occur that could make the trend line even steeper: a further increase in spending and an increase in interest rates.

So-called entitlement spending already continues to grow at alarming rates and will go even higher during an economic downturn. Interest rates, which have been relatively low for some time, inevitably will go up again. When you have a $4 trillion debt, each one percent increase in interest rates translates into an additional $40 billion a year in debt service. When rates go up, and they will, watch for deficits to balloon.

Projected Interest on the Public Debt

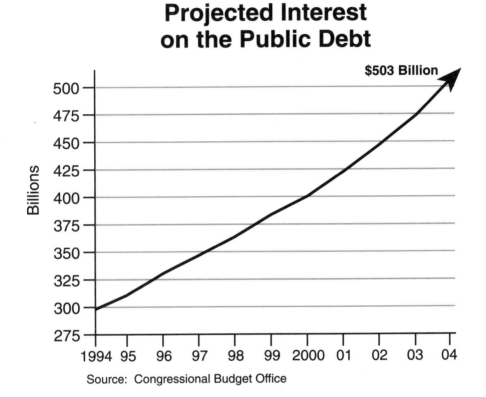

$503 Billion

Source: Congressional Budget Office

10
TREMORS

In most earthquake-prone areas, small tremors are a fact of life. I can remember the first time I felt a tremor. I was attending a meeting in southern California, and suddenly the room vibrated like an off-balance washing machine (the best analogy I could think of back then). It lasted less than a second; then it was gone.

Those of us who had never experienced tremors before were wide-eyed. But the native Californians never even put their coffee cups down. I can remember thinking, *These people are too blasé. Those rumblings are a warning of greater things to come.*

Earth tremors are an indication of unstable geological forces. In a way, they are good because they relieve some of the stresses building up. But the inhabitants must never forget that they are also warnings not to build fragile homes in a fault area.

As the tremors build in intensity, the warnings should be attended carefully. In an actual earthquake, not much can be done except to follow emergency procedures. But, in the case of an economic earthquake, changes could be made to relieve the stresses, but only if enough people are aware and *demand* action.

The following are presented as tremors signaling the excessive buildup of economic stress.

TREMOR NUMBER 1:
THE SAVINGS AND LOAN COLLAPSE

Tremors often rumble past us, giving warnings of greater catastrophes to come if no changes are made. The Savings and Loan debacle is just one of these. The total effect on the economy has yet to be felt. Essentially it is twofold: the immediate effect is a direct cost to the taxpayers of some $150 billion to cover the losses suffered by insured depositors. Some of this cost will eventually be recovered by selling off the assets held by the Resolution Trust Corporation (RTC).

A look into the S&L industry collapse is a glimpse at a typical government-enhanced debacle. During the eighties the government encouraged the S&Ls to loosen their loan standards to stimulate economic growth, particularly in the construction industry. At the same time, the 1982 tax changes gave huge tax benefits to private investors to encourage them to risk their money in new real estate ventures. The combination of these two incentives stimulated an unprecedented commercial real estate boom throughout most of the eighties.

Without question, there were some crooks and thieves in the S&L business, attracted by the looser regulations and profits to be made. But the majority of the S&Ls were run by honest business people who were responding to the direction provided from Washington. Although few senators and congressmen will admit endorsing the plan now, they certainly did when their constituents were prospering from it during the Reagan administration.

The Tax Reform Act, passed in 1986, brought with it sweeping tax changes designed to "soak the rich." A part of the new law changed the rules for real estate tax incentives—retroactively. In other words, the government reneged on the agreement that it had made with investors, which allowed them to use real estate tax shelters to offset some of their ordinary income. As a result, investors pulled out of the real estate development business—*en masse*. Existing partnerships that required additional annual payments saw investors default rather than put any more money into the projects.

Consequently, many commercial projects became insolvent, and along with them some of the S&Ls that had partially or fully backed the projects. There is no doubt that some of the previous tax laws were ill-conceived and did little more than promote overbuilding. But a deal is a deal, and when the government reneges on a contract it has made, the result is a further eroding of public trust. I knew of several politicians who spoke out against the retroactive application of the new tax changes. Their comments fell on deaf ears in the Congress and White House because politicians feared being aligned with the rich against the poor.

(This same mentality prevailed in President Clinton's tax bill. It is as if being successful in our country is a crime that must be punished. The 1993 income tax hike was passed retroactively to January 1st, before Clinton was even sworn in! It is small wonder that businesspeople feel they no longer can rely on the contracts issued by Washington.)

During the Bush administration, even more stringent regulations were applied to S&Ls in an apparent attempt to placate screaming politicians who were bent on blaming somebody else. As a result, even larger numbers of S&Ls could not meet the new solvency requirements.

As soon as this information reached the public, there was a predictable reaction: panic. Once the panic began, the S&L industry was doomed. As mentioned earlier, no banking system is safer than the public thinks it is, and the public was convinced that S&Ls in general were unsafe.

As you probably realize, about the only S&Ls that still exist are those that now call themselves Savings Banks. They fall under the control of the Federal Reserve System and are insured through the FDIC. Isn't it interesting that virtually all financial institutions, other than credit unions, now fall under the system mandated by the Keynesian economists?

TREMOR NUMBER 2:
THE BANKS

For several years, keen-eyed accountants have been warning that some of the biggest banks in America were in financial trouble. Banks like Chase Manhattan, New York City Bank, Chicago Bank and Trust, Bank of America, and dozens of others have been making loans that no prudent investor would ever have made with personal funds. Loans were made to Mexico, Brazil, Argentina, Yugoslavia, and Donald Trump—all of which were in trouble right from the beginning.

When an audit is done on most of the big banks in the country, it reads like a case study in "Banking 101" on what *not* to do with other people's money. You may recall what was mentioned earlier: depositors aren't especially watchful of the loans their banks are making, because their deposits are "protected" by a national insurance plan—the FDIC.

According to a 1990 audit done on the nation's banks, there are some 435 banks that are insolvent by *any* accounting standards. Among these are some of the largest banks, representing nearly $2 trillion in depositors' funds. Each dollar on deposit is a potential debt for the government if a bank fails. The FDIC is obligated to repay all depositors up to $100,000 per account.

The profit margins in the insurance industry have declined as the companies have had to get more competitive.

In fact, so far the FDIC has covered *all* deposits, regardless of the amount, in the large banks that have failed, such as The Republic Bank of Dallas, Chicago's Continental Illinois Bank, and the Bank of New England. The reason is simple: the government fears that if any depositors lose money in a large bank's failure there could be a run on the deposits of other large banks that would spark a major bank collapse. After all, any bank is only as safe as you or I think it is.

Since the peak of the banking crisis in 1990, the situation has eased somewhat. When interest rates fell in 1991, the profitability of most banks improved dramatically since they had to pay less for the money they borrowed, relative to what they could charge for loans themselves.

This is both good news and bad news. Banks are making more short-term profit, which helps ease their losses on investment real estate loans, but many are issuing long-term, low-interest mortgage loans that can come back to haunt them—just as they did when the S&Ls' interest rates spiraled up.

TREMOR NUMBER 3:
THE INSURANCE INDUSTRY

In the first part of this book I mentioned that one of the selling features of the insurance industry is that no major insurance company failed during the Great Depression. But the economy of the nineties is not the economy of the thirties, and a great many insurance companies are in financial trouble—some because of imprudent investments in things like junk bonds but, over all, more are in trouble because of business and real estate loans they made when times were good.

The profit margins in the insurance industry have declined as the companies have had to get more competitive. The growth of mutual funds and the onslaught of term insurance companies have pulled cash out of many of the lower-paying, whole-life plans. Also, many life insurance companies have branched out into the health insurance field and are facing rapidly declining margins of profit (or even large losses).

For decades, the whole-life (cash value) insurance companies, which represent the backbone of the industry, benefited from decreasing mortality rates as Americans lived longer. This helped the profit margins on older policies that were priced according to earlier mortality tables. These profits faded as increased competition forced most companies to adapt to the newer mortality tables and thus lower the costs of life insurance. Now many companies are looking at potentially devastating losses from early deaths due to the AIDS epidemic.

Another crisis is looming as our government attempts to "socialize" health care. There will be a few big winners among the major health insurance companies—those that survive. But there will be thousands of companies impacted and at least 140,000 health insurance agents who may find their incomes curtailed —drastically.

If the economy were growing robustly, much of the commercial real estate surplus now held by insurance companies could be resold, or at least rented out, but the economy is not robust, and the crisis in the insurance industry is a long way from over. The current uptick in the economy represents a temporary reprieve, not a pardon.

TREMOR NUMBER 4: RETIREMENT ACCOUNTS

Our generation is emotionally dependent on retirement. We have come to expect retirement as an "entitlement," unlike any generation before us. To some extent retirement is beneficial, particularly at a time when most people live longer, because through retirement older workers cycle out of the economy and make way for younger ones.

But that small benefit is negated by the loss of millions of mature workers who, although they may not be able to work harder, certainly have learned to work smarter. However, this book is not on the advisability of retirement, so I will focus on the economic impact of retirement.

The truth is, large-scale retirement is extremely expensive and becomes impossible to fund on a current basis from Social Security taxes. A large reserve is needed from which retirement benefits can be drawn since there will not be sufficient current income to cover expenses in the next decade. The Social Security Trust Fund established to meet this need is a farce; *there is no money in the fund—only government IOUs.*

The more logical element in Congress has long realized that Americans had better put something aside for their latter years.

Private retirement accounts (IRAs, 401[k]s) were designed to do just that.

The funds being put into *private* retirement accounts are beneficial from two aspects. They are a form of voluntary savings, and the majority of these funds are reinvested into the economy. It is the very success of private retirement plans that may be their downfall.

The Social Security side of retirement is detrimental to our economy—both short term and long term. Social Security "contributions" now nearly equal the total personal income taxes paid by all American workers. The impact of this on the economy is staggering, especially when you consider that the annual Social Security surpluses, now averaging some $60 to $70 billion a year, are going to feed the annual budget deficits. This strips the economy of badly needed resources. The long-term impact may be even more devastating because millions of Americans are totally dependent on Social Security to meet their retirement goals. This it cannot do simply because the tax base is declining in proportion to the retirement base. Simply put, there will be too many retirees for the workers to support.

The simple truth is: Social Security is going to be disastrously underfunded by the year 2010, as the baby boomers start to retire. Even with an increase in Social Security taxes up to 25 percent (from the present approximately 15 percent), the system is underfunded.

According to the 1992 report from the Social Security Board of Trustees, the system needs an immediate tax increase, a higher retirement age, and more taxpayers. Since raising taxes on the middle income is politically unpopular, and since abortions will have eliminated nearly 50 million potential taxpayers, the government will have to look elsewhere for the funds it will need to feed the Social Security system. The funds won't be found in the Social Security trust account. As I said earlier, those funds are gone—spent on the annual budget. In order to pay them back, the government would have to raise more taxes.

Is there a way to salvage the system? Given the political clout of the retired Americans, a way will be found; only most younger workers probably won't like it.

WHERE WILL THE MONEY COME FROM?

The answer to this question should concern any thinking American. There are actually two potential sources of new entitlement funds (other than printing the money): raise the retirement age and tap private retirement accounts.

There are millions of retired ex-federal employees drawing not only their federal retirement income but also Social Security benefits. The system is designed so that a retired worker from a career field not covered under the Social Security system can work for an additional ten years in a career that is covered, pay into Social Security the minimum contribution required, and draw benefits for a lifetime. With a contribution of no more than $7,000, a retired government employee can draw as much as $120,000 from the system, not including Medicare benefits.

Those who can qualify include members of the Congress (whose federal wages were exempt from Social Security), retired military personnel, federal government retirees, state government retirees, and exempt nonprofit organization employees (hospitals, churches, and the like). Many of these groups were brought under the Social Security system in the 1986 tax changes, but millions of previously exempt workers are now approaching retirement. By the time the workers who have paid into the system all their lives retire (from the year 2000 on) the system will be broke—twice over.

By the way, current estimates reflect that the federal employees' retirement system is underfunded by approximately $1 trillion also. Our government has been handing out IOUs on future income like a chronic gambler in Las Vegas.

Based on the need to further modify Social Security retirement, I believe it is quite possible that we will see the minimum retirement age raised to 70 before the end of this decade. I also believe we will see Social Security taxes raised, but it will not be enough to "fill the gap."

If the trust funds were intact, it is quite possible that the system would support the retirees who were born before 1938. But, there is no money, only IOUs, regardless of what our politicians proclaim. And if you believe that younger workers can pay 25 to 40 percent of their wages to support older workers, just look around at the growing resentment now. By the year 2000 there will be only 3.2 workers for every retiree.

The last alternative is one I believe will be necessary to continue the system. Bear in mind that all of these suppositions assume a growing, viable economy. At present all the facts point to anything but that. If millions of workers are unemployed, the shortfalls in every category will become much larger.

Although the federal government has not seen fit to store the surplus funds paid into the Social Security system, there is a large larder of funds available. It's called private retirement accounts.

There's approximately $4 to $5 trillion stored in pension, profit-sharing, and retirement accounts as of 1993. That is nearly equal to the shortfall in the Social Security system over the next 30 years.

Based on suggestions released to the press about using public pension funds for social projects, and the fact that the Pension Benefit Guarantee Corporation (PBGC) now insures many private pension funds, I believe retirement accounts will eventually be tapped to "supplement" Social Security contributions.

Obviously this would be illegal and contrary to all contract law. But precedent indicates that the law is ignored when it is economically expedient to do so. Our look at recent actions verifies this fact. The rules were changed when necessity dictated it. You can be assured that this vast store of money in the hands of the "wealthy" has not been overlooked in the strategy of our policy makers.

Perhaps I am wrong. I sincerely hope so. But I personally would not do my planning based on either Social Security or tax-deductible retirement accounts.

It is also possible that before the need for retirement funds gets acute, the need for more spending in the economy will get larger. If so, the laws governing the use of retirement funds for education, buying homes, or even automobiles will be changed. If they are, I would suggest using those retirement account funds in place of current income to buy a home or educate your children. Then take your current income, pay the taxes, and store it for retirement. We are a long way from the confiscation of personal assets, but remember that tax-deferred funds are not yours: they are a gift from the government (at least in their thinking). The more indigestible (unable to absorb) you make your retirement funds, the safer they will be. Basically the Social Security system can't use your house, your cars, or your kids.

THE HEALTH CARE DEFICITS

Since there is a significant movement in the Clinton administration to socialize our present health care system, I will defer this discussion to the chapters in Part II of this book.

But before closing this chapter, let me say that if the federal government is allowed to take control of health care, which represents approximately 14 percent of our total economy, it will be the stake in the heart of our free enterprise system. The government cannot solve our health care problems—it *is* the problem!

Only twelve cents of every government dollar spent on health care now actually reaches a patient. It is a grossly inefficient system.

There are two old sayings in Washington that describe what will happen to health care as soon as the political system gains control of that area too: "A camel is a horse designed by a government committee," and "An elephant is a mouse designed to government specifications." Unfortunately, these humorous quips have an uneasy ring of truth about them.

11

DEFLATION OR INFLATION?

I t is quite possible we will see a deflationary cycle in America. If allowed to run its course, this deflation could help to re-stabilize our economy. But in the face of ever-increasing federal deficits and falling revenues, it is more likely that the government will resort to even more credit, creating a massive inflationary spiral. The worst of all economic situations occurs when employment falls while prices soar.

The following is a quote from Malcolm Forbes, Jr. (publisher of *Forbes* magazine), speaking about the economic situation in Russia, but his comments would apply to any country facing potential hyperinflation.

"As those of you who have studied history know, hyperinflation is the great benefactor for dictators and tyrants. It was hyperinflation that made possible communism in Russia . . . fascism in Italy, Nazism in Germany, and then communism again in China in the mid-1940s. Hyperinflation is the enemy of democracy and reform." (Empower America Conference, December 1993)

There is a strong argument in economic circles that the U.S. economy will enter a deflationary phase during which prices will actually fall and the economy will slow significantly. The winners in such an economy are those with cash and those who are debt free. In contrast, an inflationary economy benefits the borrowers and promotes greater indebtedness.

But why would anyone believe our bloated economy is going to deflate when there has been so much debt-funded expansion during the past two decades?

That is exactly why a period of deflation is anticipated. By and large, Americans are knowledgeable, independent-minded people. When they have exceeded their borrowing limits and sense a slowdown in the economy, they traditionally cut back on borrowing, concentrate on repaying some of what they owe, and generally get more conservative financially.

This trend has changed somewhat because a whole generation has been born into prosperity (and indebtedness), and unfortunately a whole generation has been raised to expect government handouts. But for the most part, many traditional values still exist within the younger generation too.

In spite of the alarming statistics on personal bankruptcies, most Americans will sacrifice to repay their debts, including selling unnecessary assets in bad times if required.

You don't have to look much farther than Texas to see what can happen to home prices during a severe economic slowdown.

Several factors point toward a period of deflation in our economy.

First, we have just about pushed the limit on debt-funded housing. Over the past two decades home prices have escalated to the point that the average home buyer cannot afford to buy the average home. To provide the extra income needed to qualify for the more costly homes, many women made a mass exodus from their homes to the workplace during the seventies and eighties. But this has leveled off now, and a lot of women are opting to settle for less expensive houses so they can stay home with their children.

If this trend continues as expected, home prices should drop over the next few years or at least level out to some degree. This should result in a deflationary period for the second largest industry in our country. It will be good news for new buyers, but bad news for those using their homes as revolving lines of credit.

You don't have to look much farther than Texas to see what can happen to home prices during a severe economic slowdown. I know a couple who exemplify what can happen to anyone.

Cal and Andrea lived in Houston, Texas, where Cal managed a retail department store. Andrea worked for an attorney specializing in legal work for the oil industry.

Prior to the Arab oil embargo in the early seventies, Cal and Andrea had lived in Oklahoma, where Cal managed a similar but smaller store. When oil prices shot up and the Texas economy expanded rapidly, Cal's company asked him to relocate to Houston to manage a new store. He accepted the offer and, since the new position involved a bigger store and a higher salary, he and Andrea felt they could afford a better home.

They moved to Houston in 1974 and purchased a four-bedroom, three-bath home in a nice neighborhood for $157,000. By 1975 the booming economy in Houston had driven the price of similar homes in their area up to nearly $250,000. Virtually every home was sold before construction was finished.

They borrowed against the equity in their home to install a swimming pool and landscape the property. Even so, the combined mortgages were only $190,000, and the payments were well within their combined incomes.

Then in 1980 disaster struck the oil industry as prices fell to pre-embargo levels. Cal noticed a significant drop in the volume of his store, even though it was a well-established discount store. The parent company was also shocked by the drop in sales, so prices were slashed to near break-even levels in an attempt to ride out what everyone believed was a temporary situation.

By 1982 it was apparent that the oil business in general was in trouble and the decline would not be as temporary as everyone had thought. Cal was fortunate because the parent company he worked for had the resources to ride out the downturn and was willing to do so, so he kept his job. But Andrea was not as fortunate; her employer was directly tied to the oil business, and in early 1983 she lost her job.

With the drop in income and few comparable positions available, they decided they had to sell their home. They both knew the Houston real estate market was down, but neither had any idea just how bad it was. They put their home on the market for $240,000 and had absolutely no offers. In fact, they had no lookers.

> *Deflation can be a great asset for those with cash to invest.*

Over the next year they reduced the price several times, until they reached their break-even point on the outstanding loans: $190,000. Still they had no offers and very few lookers.

Andrea decided to do some checking on her own, so she began to call about some of the homes for sale in their community. What she discovered shocked her. The average price of a comparable home being offered (by the owner) was $140,000. But similar homes being offered by those who had already moved out of the state to find work averaged about $110,000.

Although bargains, these were not the lowest priced homes being offered. Foreclosed homes similar to theirs were being offered by the mortgage companies for as little as $80,000! In addition, the lenders were offering discounted interest rates, additional home equity loans—even trips to the Bahamas to qualified buyers.

By the end of 1983, long before the economy of Texas began a gradual turnaround, average home prices in their community dropped to as low as $100,000. But by 1985, if Cal and Andrea had been able to return their home to the mortgage company, they could have bought a similar home for $40,000 with a 15-year, 8 percent mortgage and only 10 percent down . . . and it had a larger pool.

Deflation can be a great asset for those with cash to invest. I know of an investor who bought dozens of homes in the Texas and Oklahoma area during this period. The homes he paid $40,000 or less for are now selling for $100,000 or more. Prices still have not returned to the pre-crash level and probably will not for several years, but the economy has returned to some semblance of normalcy.

THE MECHANICS OF DEFLATION

The second deflationary factor occurs when prices exceed the ability of the average consumer to buy what is offered. Demand can be artificially stimulated by lowering interest rates until consumers are enticed to buy again, in which case they are buying based on the perceived value of the loan, *not* necessarily the product. The "no interest" car loans of the late eighties are a good example of this. Many people bought cars they couldn't afford, simply because the loan was perceived as too good to pass up.

If allowed to run its full course, a deflationary spiral in the U.S. would wipe out millions of jobs. In the case of the deflation in Texas, there were jobs elsewhere for many of the displaced workers since the overall U.S. economy was doing well. But in a nationwide deflation, there would be widespread unemployment. Often the jobs that are available during a deflationary period are lower-paying, public service jobs. These types of jobs help to keep food on the table, but they won't pay the mortgage payments for most families.

A look at the most recent deflationary cycle will help give a better perspective of what happens when the downturn is broader and more pronounced.

As noted earlier, the 1980s saw the greatest credit-generated boom in American history. Businesses borrowed to expand; the government borrowed to expand; and consumers borrowed to expand. The automobile industry is a classic example of what can be called "smoke and mirrors" economics.

By the mid-eighties automobile prices had escalated to the point that most average buyers could not afford a new car. To overcome consumers' reluctance to spend more than they could afford, the automobile industry introduced "no interest loans." Anyone with common sense knows that you don't get something for nothing, so the industry had to build enough profit into the car prices to cover the loss of interest. But buyers did respond, and car sales soared. When Ronald Reagan left office, the great debt binge of the eighties slowed greatly. Buyers woke up to the fact that they had to pay their "no interest" car loans back. Consequently car sales plummeted, adding to the recession of 1990.

Lower interest rates since 1991 have allowed many families and businesses to renegotiate older, high-interest loans. This has had a positive effect on the economy. But now (1994) we are seeing a disturbing trend developing as families are loading up on consumer debt once again.

This cycle seems to repeat itself after every recession. People get desperate to reduce their debt load when they see family and friends lose their jobs. But as soon as the cycle reverses, they go right back to their former habits.

If I could offer one piece of counsel, it would be to avoid this trap. The uptick in our economy is not based on any solid foundation, nor are the cut backs in industry over by any means. Once the effect of the Clinton tax increases hit our economy, it is very likely we will experience another recession right on the heels of the last one.

Statistically, there is little doubt that our economy is in a long-term deflationary cycle, as I suggested it would be when *The Coming Economic Earthquake* was first published in 1991. Take this opportunity to refinance any high-interest loans at the lower rates, but then continue to pay at the same rate as before and this can be an excellent opportunity to get out of debt—totally!

WHY A RECESSION?

Often I have been asked why I think that the mid-nineties will be deflationary. The answer is fairly simple: a sinking economy. We have loaded this economy with two of the biggest tax increases in history (1991 and 1993). There is simply no way to remove so much spendable income from the hands of consumers without having a negative economic effect—that is unless Bill Clinton really has rewritten the text books on economics.

In addition to the tax increases, our president and the Congress also have agreed to lower carbon dioxide emissions in industry back to 1990 levels. This will cost millions of jobs and will shut down some major industries—or at least force them to spend hundreds of billions of dollars unproductively. This is to solve a problem (global warming) that virtually no reputable scientists believe exists.

On top of this, the Clinton administration is vigorously enforcing environmental legislation on everything from wetlands to gnat catchers. These regulations are nothing less than another tax that will have to be paid by every American worker.

But the biggest fraud of all time is underway. It is called the great-hole-in-the-ozone scare. To protect the ozone from its mythical demise by chlorofluorocarbon (CFC) emissions, our government has agreed to phase out the production and use of all CFCs by 1996. The most common use of CFCs is in freon, the basic refrigerant for virtually all of the cooling systems in the world. It is estimated that the cost to consumers to replace all of the existing cooling systems in America alone will cost about $2 trillion (that's *trillion*).

It is unbelievable that anyone would actually attempt to do this on little more than "voodoo" science promoted by environmental extremists. But such action at this particular time in our economy goes beyond the realm of madness. This will cause massive disruptions in every industry, as well as in the lives of every American family. These costs will be passed along in the form of higher prices for virtually everything we buy: food, medicine, cars, homes, and so on. But even more than this, it establishes a trend toward environmental extremism that can shut down the U.S. economy.

In case you might think I am exaggerating the problem, I would refer you to the *What Ever Happened to the American Dream* book (Moody Press). This issue and several other lesser frauds being perpetrated on the American people are well documented. If you listen only to the national media, you might get the impression that global destruction is imminent and verifiable. I can assure you this is not the case.

All of this is taking place just as we are recovering from a recession. As I said when *The Coming Economic Earthquake* book was first published, I thought the recession of 1990-91 would officially end in early 1992. Actually, it ended officially in early 1991, even though the media distorted the facts during the campaign of 1992 to help Bill Clinton get elected. Therefore, he inherited an economy which was recovering from the worst of the recession.

It is again my opinion that the recovery probably will carry us well into 1994 before the effects of the Clinton tax increase is felt in the economy. That, along with the previously mentioned attempts to eliminate freon and lower carbon dioxide emissions, should send the economy spiraling down—perhaps into an abyss.

When the health care plan is placed on the backs of small businesses, there is a high probability that we will see a significant economic downturn of much longer duration. Is this to be the depression of the 1990s? No one can really say. We'll just have to wait and see how well the economy can absorb these blows.

I must admit that I am continually impressed at how resilient our economy is. Most assuredly it's resilience comes from the sound biblical principles upon which it was founded and operated —until recently. If we could just get the government back into its proper role and allow the free enterprise system to function as it was intended, possibly we could recover even from the pit we are digging for ourselves.

THE 1994 ELECTIONS

Perhaps more than anything else, the 1994 elections will signal the direction that our economy will take long-term. If Americans decide to kick out enough of the Socialists (liberals, or whatever you call them) and elect men and women who are pledged to reducing the size and scope of the federal government, then just maybe we still have a chance to recover before a total economic collapse. But if American voters decide to reelect the bigger government advocates who will in turn support the Health Security Act, more regulatory controls, and more debt to fund it all, then the future bodes ill for all of us.

Before Bill Clinton was elected I thought things could not get worse. In fact, I honestly thought that Americans would begin to demand less government meddling into their lives. After all, virtually everything the government has touched thus far has gotten more expensive, less efficient, and more complicated.

The whole phenomenon of Ross Perot was centered around the need to reduce the federal budget and the size of government. It is one of those quirks of fate that Perot's candidacy may have pulled enough swing votes away from George Bush that Bush lost the election. At any rate, Americans ended up with a president whose basic values run almost opposite those of the majority (those who voted for Bush and Perot).

If in the '94 elections the voters don't make some significant changes and send a signal to Washington to back off, in my opinion we will most assuredly see a significant swing toward more debt and government programs.

If the elections of '94 confirm Clinton's policies, I would change my previous estimate of an economic collapse from near the turn of the century to '96-'98.

12

EARLY INDICATORS

I need to emphasize once again that there are no "absolutes" when it comes to economic forecasting. We live in a society where few people want to live by absolutes themselves but they want others to provide them with absolute answers. If that's what you expected when you picked up this book, I'm sorry, but you're going to be disappointed. I think I can offer some guidelines or indicators of what to look for in our economy, but absolutes are the sole realm of God.

POSITIVE INDICATORS

It is a possibility, however remote, that our government leaders will recognize the dangerous path they are on and decide to get fiscally responsible.

I don't mean to imply that no one in Washington understands the crisis we face or wants to do anything about it. There are many financially conservative politicians who also believe the government is on a collision course with disaster and needs to change immediately. Unfortunately they are a minority and are often characterized by the more fiscally liberal politicians as uncaring right-wingers, which in itself is ridiculous because many of these people are among those labeled as socially liberal themselves by most political conservatives.

Representative among this group are two politicians who were in Congress a few years ago: Congresswoman Millicent Fenwick and Senator William Proxmire. No one has ever accused either of them of being "conservatives," but both spoke out strongly against waste and debt during their tenure in Washington.

POSITIVE INDICATOR 1: INITIATE SPENDING CUTS

If the Congress decides to follow the law as set down by the Gramm-Rudman Act, the 1990 Budget Enforcement Act, and the 1993 Omnibus Budget Reconciliation Act, and reduces the federal budget enough to make it balance by 1998, you will know that the economy is headed down the path to recovery. In truth, we all know this will not happen without at least a 50 percent change-over in Congress.

> *It is often too easy to blame the Congress for everything because they are the "big" spenders.*

There simply is no way to bring the budget into balance and exclude 70 percent of current spending. This action would bring those in Congress who are dedicated to the redistribution of wealth screaming to the media. The political nature of this issue makes implementation almost impossible.

POSITIVE INDICATOR 2: STOP THE "PORK BARREL" POLITICS

If the Congress allows the president a line-item veto so that he can reject specific areas of overspending without rejecting the entire budget, you will know they're serious about solving the problems.

As it is now, the Congress attaches hundreds of special-interest provisions to appropriation bills. The overall bill may be associated with a politically sensitive issue, such as civil rights or aid for dependent children. The president is then confronted with either giving his okay to the bill (including the pork barrel spending) or rejecting the entire bill, causing a political backlash. If the politicians decide to stop this pork barrel method of funding their special projects, you'll know they are serious.

POSITIVE INDICATOR 3: STOP
THE DIVERSION OF NON-BUDGET FUNDS

If the president will decide to stop robbing funds from Social Security and will allow the budget to reflect the true deficits, including the off-budget entitlement programs, you will know the executive branch is also serious about solving the country's economic problem.

We have a system that bogs down under stress and leaders who are more concerned with avoiding the blame than solving the problems.

It is often too easy to blame the Congress for everything because they are the "big" spenders. But the executive branch of our political system has pushed its pet projects too. When you see members of the White House staff driving their own cars to work and flying the commercial airlines like the rest of us, then you'll know the executive branch is serious too.

POSITIVE INDICATOR 4: FORM A
GOVERNMENT/BUSINESS PARTNERSHIP TO EXPAND EXPORTS

One economic factor that could signal an improving market for American goods is the expansion into eastern Europe by American businesses. This vast untapped market lacks the capital to buy many Western goods presently. But they will certainly emerge as a viable economic force before the end of this century, bringing 100 million new and willing consumers on line. This market base could enhance the U.S. economy to the point where we could absorb the present debt (assuming the politicians stop future waste). If the U.S. waits, we will find ourselves trying to catch up with the Asians in Europe, as we have in our own country. By the end of the century the Russians should have recovered sufficiently to be formidable competitors (or enemies) also.

NEGATIVE INDICATORS

While I sincerely pray that our leaders will show enough statesmanship and courage to make these changes and more, I seriously doubt that our political system will support such an effort.

No long-range changes are possible unless some short-range sacrifices are made by the American people. I question that our generation has the will and determination (or foresight) to back those who would do what is best in the long run.

Perhaps I am wrong. I sincerely pray that I am because I live in this country too. However, to date I have not seen many leaders with the integrity of a Grover Cleveland or an Abraham Lincoln, who will do what is best for the country regardless of the political consequences.

The decisions that must be made, once the cracks in the economy begin to widen, require swift and positive leadership. In my opinion, we have a system that bogs down under stress and leaders who are more concerned with avoiding the blame than solving the problems. As a result, when the real economic tremors begin, it will be too late to do much about it. The mentality of my fellow Americans truly astounds me sometimes. Even with the massive debt already accumulated and annual deficits now doubling every five years, there is no real clamor for change. Apparently the average American has either bought the nonsense that the debt doesn't matter, or they simply don't care.

I trust that some do, and that you are one of them. The collapse of this economy truly will come like "a thief in the night." Trying to bolt the doors after the thief is inside is a rather fruitless effort.

NEGATIVE INDICATOR 1: THE DEFICIT
CANNOT BE FUNDED BY ADDITIONAL BORROWING

Up to the time of this writing, our government has been able to avoid the consequences of hyperinflation because the annual deficits have been funded through loans.

Once the limit to which foreign investors will fund the U.S. debt is reached, a monetary crisis is not far off.

Some inflation does occur even when the deficits are funded this way because the fractional banking system creates some new money, based on the multiplier effect previously discussed. However, the amount of fiat money this system can create is insignificant in comparison to the deficits of the federal government. The fractional banking system is limited to multiplying only the deposits on hand. As these dry up, the money supply shrinks proportionately. The net result is a nagging 4 or 6 percent inflation rate, which is bad but not when compared with that of the other countries we discussed, which simply printed the money they needed.

Two points must be noted here. First, the countries where hyperinflation ignited so quickly lacked the established credit rating of the United States. Hence, they simply had to start printing money to cover their deficits much sooner.

The second point is that *any* debt-funded economy will eventually exhaust its available credit. If allowed to grow unchecked, the annual deficits will exceed the total funds available from all sources.

The competition between the government and businesses for available funds is a real concern to most economists who understand that the total funds available to both the public and private sector are limited. The more money the government pulls out of the system to feed its own spending, the less that is available for businesses. Since only the government can support the enormous deficits it has, businesses are in constant jeopardy of losing their source of capital.

The following graph depicts the needs of businesses and government for annual loans. As you can see, the more the government siphons off, the less that is available for all others. The law of supply and demand eventually comes into play, and the price of credit climbs beyond the reach of the productive side of our economy.

Effect of Federal Budget Deficit on National Savings

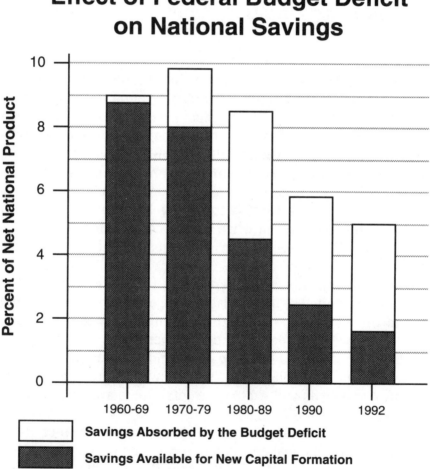

Savings Absorbed by the Budget Deficit

Savings Available for New Capital Formation

Source: Economic Report of the President, Feb. 1992

Based on the projected deficits, this point will be reached sometime in the latter part of this decade. Unless the government reduces its demand for capital, the business base of American industry will eventually be forced to sell out to foreign investors to acquire the needed funds.

This is one of the indicators I mentioned earlier. When the annual deficits (on budget and off) reach the level where the government can no longer fund them without taking critical operating funds away from industry, the economic blow-off is not far away.

The printing of money with no equity backing is essentially counterfeiting by the government.

How can you know when this is happening? Just read *The Wall Street Journal* or *Investor's Business Daily*, or listen to the news on one of the financial cable channels. I can assure you there are professional analysts who make their living monitoring the money supply. They will signal this crisis well in advance. I personally would disregard any verbal contradictions coming out of Washington. (This also applies to the media if they feel the information might hurt their social agenda.) However, the statistical data published by the Federal Reserve accurately reflects the nation's financial status—thus far.

NEGATIVE INDICATOR 2: MONETIZING THE DEBT

There is an urgent need for a federal law prohibiting the printing of additional currency to cover any budget shortfalls. Without such a law (carrying stiff penalties) there is little incentive to balance the budget. As long as the government has an "out" there will always be the temptation to use it. The printing of money with no equity backing is essentially counterfeiting by the government. Let me assure you we will never hear the economic policy makers voice the following message: "Attention Americans. Today we will start monetizing the national debt. You can expect extremely high levels of inflation to follow."

Instead, an innocuous term such as monetary equalization will be used. This is what George Orwell described as "newspeak" in his novel, *Nineteen Eighty-Four*.

We are usually told by campaigning politicians that no new taxes will be allowed while they are in office. Then a few months later, when you receive your tax bill, it looks like you owe more taxes this year than you did last year, but your income remained the same. Why?

The political explanation: You didn't have a tax increase; you experienced a "revenue enhancement." A revenue enhancement often means that we taxpayers lost some of the deductions so generously granted to us in previous years. The net effect is the same: More of our incomes are transferred to the government. A little later we'll look at some of the more probable revenue enhancers.

> *Treasury securities now in circulation have no real collateral behind them other than the holder's confidence in our government.*

When debt is "monetized," it simply means that a new form of currency has been issued as legal tender. This was done in the 1700s when the fledgling American government issued scrip to replace the British pound. Later the highly devalued scrip was exchanged for the continental dollar. A few years later the continental dollar was so worthless, due to indiscriminate printing, that it was exchanged for U.S. gold or silver certificates. As long as the dollar was backed by these metals, there was very little inflation.

The New Deal administration exchanged the gold certificates for Federal Reserve notes, allowing the dollar to rise and fall, depending on the state of the economy.

Then in the sixties, the use of base metal coins was substituted for silver coins, effectively removing all fixed asset value from U.S. currency.

So the precedent is well established for the additional monetizing of our currency. Only this time it probably will be the printing of a currency already in circulation: the dollar. Simply put, we will eventually be forced to print what we can't borrow.

The Treasury securities now in circulation have no real collateral behind them other than the holder's confidence in our government. Those who hold U.S. dollars throughout the world are reasonably sure that the government will not print additional bills without removing the equivalent number from circulation. If they thought otherwise they (including you and I) would dump or trade our currency as quickly as possible. Because each new bill printed and put into circulation would make those we are holding worth less than before.

Think of the dollars you hold like stock in a company. Suppose a company with a total worth of $100,000 is authorized to issue 100 shares of stock. So you buy one share with assurance that it's worth $1,000, based on the current value of the company. Later the company needs more capital, so the directors issue 100 more shares and sell them to the public for $1,000 a share.

At first glance, you might think, *Well, it doesn't hurt me. I still have my share worth $1,000.*

But is it really worth $1,000? If the company is still valued at $100,000 and there are 200 shares outstanding, your share is only worth $500. However, it is possible that no one else knows that another 100 shares have been issued. The "logical" thing to do in that case is to dump your shares before the others discover the company has diluted your stock by 50 percent.

In the case of a public company that did this, the directors would be subject to both civil lawsuits and criminal prosecution because they violated the securities law and the trust agreement with their original stockholders. It is unfortunate that the same rules do not apply to governments and their dollar holders.

The current method of funding the government's debt is that the Treasury issues loan agreements (T-bills, bonds, and the like), which are sold through the Federal Reserve banks strategically located throughout the country. Since each issue from the Treasury is a sale of securities, the laws applicable to public information require total disclosure.

In the event the Treasury decides to print fiat money to pay the government's bills, you can be sure the action will be cloaked in secrecy and disguised as something else, contrary to the securities' laws. But I have confidence that the American free enterprise system will not allow such activities to go unnoticed or unreported.

It should be noted here that the printing of money to pay the government's bills will be one of the last, and certainly the most desperate, measures because of the potential severity of the consequences.

Additional taxes take away the ability to save for future generations.

On the other hand, the money managers may counsel that it's okay to print a little money along the way to ease the demand on the money supply.

I am reminded that eighty years ago the money managers promised that the federal income tax would never exceed 2 percent of earned income.

NEGATIVE INDICATOR 3: TAXES, TAXES, TAXES . . .

When the American standard of living is compared to that of most other countries of the world, it is evident that we can support much higher tax rates. Even supporting a federal income tax of 50 percent would not require a reduction in living standards as much as it would a change of lifestyles. It would necessitate a return to one car per family, multiple generations per home, less education, one suit in the closet, and so on.

If we don't wake up and demand some changes, this is exactly where we are headed again. Additional taxes take away the ability to save for future generations.

Those who support a higher tax rate point out that not too long ago the maximum tax rate in our country was 70 percent and people still lived okay. What they miss is that most taxpayers didn't fall into the highest bracket and, in fact, the tax rate was designed specifically to encourage high income individuals to invest in the economy through the use of tax shelters.

Most certainly, average-income wage earners would balk at a tax rate of 50 percent or more, so it would need to be disguised. Allow me to share some creative ways to do this.

Gasoline Tax. Congress has raised the gas tax twice in the past five years, but it's such an "easy" source of revenue that it's bound to be increased again. A proposal that is raised frequently in the Congress is assigning a "user fee" to gasoline. The general consensus is about ten cents per gallon. An alternate suggestion is 10 percent fee per gallon, which would provide an inflation hedge (for the government of course). As the cost of gasoline went up, the fee would follow. This method of tax increase is called *indexing.*

A federal gasoline tax would raise an additional $15 to $20 billion annually. Because of its impact on the lower income groups, a new tax on gasoline would probably provide some form of tax credit based on income.

Value-Added Tax (VAT). Those who have traveled through England and Europe are familiar with the value-added tax system. It is a national tax (with local government participation) that is added to each stage of material production and distribution.

In the United States, no sales taxes are added until a product is sold to the consumer. Not so in the value-added system. Each recipient of raw materials or processed materials pays a tax. The raw materials sent to a processor are taxed. Then the processed materials are taxed to the manufacturer. They are taxed again when sold to the retailer. Another percentage is added when the products are sold to the consumers.

The value-added tax (on most products) can be as high as 40 percent when the totals are accumulated. Since the tax is paid by all classes of taxpayers, the income to the government is significantly greater than a graduated income tax. But don't expect the VAT to replace the income tax. In countries which already have a value-added tax, such as England, France, and Germany, income tax rates are 40 percent or more. In some of the more socialized economies, such as Norway and Sweden, income tax rates are as high as 70 percent. Based on a complicated formula, some income is taxed at more than 100 percent. It is designed to be the optimum "soak the rich" tax.

A value-added tax on all goods and services in America could potentially add an additional $300 billion annually to the government's coffers. But it's important to remember that you don't get something for nothing. The $300 billion must be removed from the private sector economy to be given to the public sector. Doing so reduces the consumer's buying power and thus ripples through the entire economy.

> *What is the national debt but the visible indicator of gross fiscal mismanagement on the part of our leaders?*

Visualize the tax system like a home builder who wants to economize on his construction costs by removing the wall studs one at a time to see how many are really necessary to keep the walls standing. If he removes one too many, the whole structure collapses.

The government is playing the same game with money in the private sector. If it removes too much private capital, the whole structure can collapse. Unfortunately the mentality of too many Americans today is that it would *never* do that.

A National Lottery. It would seem entirely plausible that the federal government will turn to a lottery of some kind when the need for more money becomes acute. Based on what the states are able to generate through their lotteries, a national lottery would net the government about $20 to $25 billion annually. If the government gets really creative and makes the proceeds tax free, the net could be as high as $100 billion.

I hesitate to mention a national lottery lest someone in Washington who had not already thought about it pick up on the idea. But I read in a national magazine that two of our more liberal senators had already proposed the idea. Raising money through gambling represents just one more small crack in the ever-expanding financial chasm.

The "success" of state lotteries in reducing taxes should forewarn everyone that lotteries *do not* reduce taxes. The net effect is an increase in income, but at the cost of morality and more welfare to compensate for the money the poor spend on gambling.

It is important to remember that more taxes are not a problem. They are the symptom of a greater internal problem: indulgence. A politician would rather do anything other than raise taxes. The escalating growth of the national debt is evidence of this. After all, what is the national debt but the visible indicator of gross fiscal mismanagement on the part of our leaders? But rather than facing irate voters by raising the money they spend, our leaders borrow the money and put off the inevitable one more year—or day.

So when you see an increase in taxes (other than a "soak the rich" tax) you know the politicians are desperate. The more visible the tax, such as the value-added tax, the more desperate they are for money. When they dip down into the pockets of the low-income groups through taxes on food, gasoline, and medicines, the end is nearing.

13
THE FINAL WARNINGS

In one study I read describing earthquakes, a group of scientists presented some convincing evidence that animals can be used as early warning detectors.

For instance, ants seem to sense the faint rumblings of an earthquake even before the most sensitive seismology equipment can. Ant colonies begin migrating away from the areas of eruption long before there is even a hint of geological activity. Of course, since many ant colonies are in constant migration, it is easy to overlook the obvious sometimes. Only by studying stable colonies have scientists begun to accept this theory as a possible indicator.

The same can be said of the economic indicators. After all, taxes are always in a state of flux. And our currency has been changed at least twice in this century. So why worry about these indicators? It is both the intensity and the combination of many factors converging that represent the best early warning indicators.

If I lived in an earthquake area I wouldn't be particularly concerned about a migrating colony of ants. But if I woke up one morning and noticed the majority of ants packing up to move, it would get my attention. I think I would question whether they knew something I didn't. From that point on, I would be on the alert for other indicators.

The same group of scientists who noted the movement of ants prior to major eruptions also noted that many species of birds vacate the area just prior to the actual earthquake. The birds either don't have the early warning sensitivity of the ants, or they know they can escape faster. But once the time draws near, apparently they can feel the low frequency rumblings preceding the actual eruption.

The general rule in predicting earthquakes is, The earlier the better. But the absolute rule is, Any warning is better than none at all. Applying this logic to our coming economic earthquake, I believe the earlier we can spot it coming, the better it will be for all of us, especially those who will *do something* in advance. But even those who choose to ignore all the early warning indicators will be attentive when the loud rumblings start. I might not be concerned if a few ants left the area, but if I woke up to find all the animals gone, that would get my attention. There are some people, however, who would say, "Good! The noisy varmints are gone!" and then roll over and go back to sleep.

> *Our economy will suffer a shattering depression during which the government will attempt to stimulate the economy by inflating the currency.*

Those charged with the management of our economy will likely say, "That's ridiculous. There are no real problems with our economy. Roll over and go back to sleep." If you do, I believe your sleep will be rudely interrupted. As with a geological earthquake, there is little you can do once the earth begins to move, except flee your house for an open field somewhere close by. But even standing in an open field during a major quake is better than staying inside. Perhaps all you can do once the economy begins to crumble is save what you can of your assets (house, car, or the like) by paying them off; at least you'll be doing something.

Based on the study of other economic collapses, I believe there will be a series of crises prior to either a depression or hyperinflation. It is also my firm conviction that our economy will suffer a shattering depression during which the government will attempt to stimulate the economy by inflating the currency. This will then initiate a period of hyperinflation.

In order to understand how and why this can happen, we must project ourselves into the future and decide what we would do under the conditions that will be facing the president and Congress at that time. Remember, these are not "super heroes." Nor are they clairvoyant. They are people who make decisions based on the facts at hand and the political climate at the time. What Americans in the thirties expected of their government was far less than what is expected today. Ten years of depression left a lot of people disillusioned in the thirties. Today it would leave burned-out hulks of cities throughout America.

As I commented before, we're whipping our horse (the economy) to avoid the Indians chasing us (the debt). We realize if we keep inflating the economy at this pace it will collapse. But we also know that if the economy stops for any period of time, the debt will overwhelm us. So what can we do? Keep whipping our horses and hoping for miracles.

When you see cracks appearing in the earth in an earthquake zone, the actual eruption is near. When you see cracks in the economy, you'll know that financial eruption is near also.

CRACK NUMBER 1:
BANKING CRISIS

We have discussed in part the potential of a banking crisis, but one of the signs of an imminent collapse is massive bank failures. Just in case you may not be aware that there is a banking crisis looming, I need to point out some facts.

Laws used to be in place which prohibited banking corporations from owning banks across state lines. The logic behind this limitation was obvious: If one corporation controlled enough banks, it could eventually develop a monopoly and choke off the competition. But there was another reason for it. If a huge banking corporation developed financial problems, it could threaten the whole banking system.

Mergers and buy-outs work only if the surviving entity is financially stronger than those absorbed. That was not the case with many of the S&Ls, and it may not be the case with many of the "mega-banks" that are now emerging.

Larger banks do have access to the funds to buy out weaker institutions simply because of their size. But their debt-to-asset ratios are actually worse than many of the smaller banks. Unless there are some genuine efforts to bring the big banks under control, when the real economic crunch comes they will simply go under with a bigger bang.

We are witnessing the conversion of the entire banking industry into a new financial entity.

To help shore up the banking industry, watch for the government to allow non-banking corporations to own banks. That will open the door for large retailers like Sears, J.C. Penney, Wal-Mart, Kmart, and others to buy banks. Additionally it will pave the way for insurance companies and stock brokerage firms to get into the banking business.

The advantage to the non-banking corporations is obvious. It would give them access to depositors' funds at extremely low rates and access to the lucrative credit card business. For the insurance companies and brokerage firms, it would provide a nationwide outlet for their products through neighborhood banks.

The negative side is that such changes would break down the barriers between depositors and financial product marketers. It also would open the door to abuses, such as a bank making loans to the parent company. This in turn would make the banks more vulnerable to problems in the parent company's industry.

In short it would provide an instant "shot in the arm" for the banking industry, but it could easily destabilize the economy in the long run. The only thing that would make such a move possible is the federal depositors insurance program. Otherwise, nervous depositors would pull out of troubled banks, especially those making loans to their parent companies.

We are witnessing already the conversion of the entire banking industry into a new financial entity. If these mergers and acquisitions strengthen the banks, the economy will benefit. But if the big, shaky banks simply gobble up the smaller, more conservative banks to get at their asset base, it can be a critical blow to the economy.

Banks are private companies that make their money in the lending business. If the majority of their loans are participating (making their payments), then they are solvent. Once the number of bad loans exceeds the statistical number necessary to repay the depositors' interest, the banks will fail without government intervention.

In a bad economy with unemployment exceeding 10 percent or more, many of the normally sound loans will default. This crack in the economy will be highly publicized because it will swallow up hundreds of banks, large and small, and will require a *trillion dollars* or more in additional government subsidies.

Once again the same question surfaces: Where will the funds come from at a time when the economy is flagging and the government's income is declining? The same three options are available: new taxes, more loans, or printed money. Take your pick.

CRACK NUMBER 2:
BUSINESS FAILURES AND DEPARTURES

When all is said and done, the business community in our country is the heart of our economy. The single bright spot that I can see on the horizon is the ability of American entrepreneurs to adapt to virtually any situation and still make a profit.

The biggest negative is the excessive burden placed on them by our political system. It is very popular these days to attack business people as greedy money grubbers who need to be watched carefully and regulated heavily. If this trend continues, we will lose the base from which all of our capital is generated. Allow me to cite an example.

Some time ago a businessman I know called to say that he was relocating his business outside the U.S. The reason: the constant pressure from our government bureaucracy.

He owned a company in the western United States and a sizeable portion of his business was providing parts for catalytic convertors on automobiles. A part of the manufacturing process involved the use of a potent acid catalyst, which was recaptured, cleaned, and reused.

Three years earlier he was required by the Environmental Protection Agency (EPA) to install some very expensive equipment to monitor the plant's environment to ensure that no workers were exposed to the caustic fumes. He did this willingly, believing it was in the best interests of his employees.

[The EPA has] become a paramilitary enforcement group running amok throughout the free enterprise system.

Recently he received a bill from the EPA for his "share" of an environmental cleanup. It seems the company he bought the monitoring equipment from also used toxic chemicals in their testing facility. The facility failed to meet EPA standards and was required to decontaminate their entire complex, which meant chipping out several hundred yards of concrete and storing it in sealed containers for the next 150 years or so. Rather than absorb these costs, the company, a subsidiary of a foreign firm, declared bankruptcy and closed its doors.

The EPA then sent a portion of the cleanup estimate to all the companies that had ever done business with the firm, including this businessman. The thing about it that bothered him the most was the only slightly veiled threat he received. The attorneys for the EPA warned him that if he refused to pay his "share," amounting to tens of thousands of dollars, he could be held liable for the entire cleanup, amounting to several millions of dollars. The timing was significant since he had just returned from an industry meeting where other business owners shared horror stories of similar conflicts with various government agencies. Many of them had had their assets attached when they refused to comply.

"Enough is enough," he told me. "Government officials from another country want me to relocate my business there, and they've offered me tax breaks, low-interest loans, and governmental guarantees of *no* interference. I can see the handwriting on the wall here. So I'm going!"

He offered his employees a chance to relocate also. As expected, no one took the offer, so 1300 employees were out of a job, and another industry left the U.S.

I'm sure some newspaper or television station in his area will eventually do a report on the callous businessman who dumped his employees for a few dollars. But that was not the case at all. He grieved over his decision, and then he provided liberal benefits to those who were dismissed.

"My great concern," he said, "is that one day the rules will get so oppressive that I won't be able to operate profitably and laws will be passed to keep me from relocating. So I'm getting out while I still can." He saw the EPA in the same role as the KGB in Russia. They have become a paramilitary enforcement group running amok throughout the free enterprise system.

The environment has become the new buzzword in Washington, and there is little doubt that more of this kind of activity will take place.

When the additional factors of mandatory health insurance, workers' compensation, liability insurance, property taxes, inventory taxes and, eventually, value-added taxes are dumped on small and medium-sized businesses, we will see some massive failures.

The interdependent relationships between banks and businesses tend to feed each other. If one goes, the other is sure to follow.

As banks fail, the primary source of operating capital dries up for the local businesses. Then, as businesses fail, other banks are jeopardized because they have loaned to businesses that are dependent on the failed enterprises.

This may sound depressing, but perhaps making more people aware of the impending crisis will help to deal with the problems before the whole structure unravels.

CRACK NUMBER 3:
THE DENIAL SYNDROME

The one thing you can be certain of is that no one in the power structure of Washington will admit to any problems until the evidence is so overwhelming that it is obvious to all. It's like we're headed down the Niagara River in a powerless boat, and yet they still insist, "There is no problem. The sound you hear in the distance is not a waterfall. We promise!"

I heard Lee Iacocca say during an interview in the midst of the 1990 recession, "I know the politicians tell us that we're not in a recession and we're not going to be, but, from where I stand, it sure does look like a recession."

I agree with Mr. Iacocca. If it is in the best interests of the political system to deny a problem, they will do so in spite of overwhelming evidence to the contrary. The more vehement the denials, the bigger the potential crisis.

Even if the evidence indicates bank failures, business failures, and desperate efforts on the part of federal and state governments to raise funds, you can be sure the information coming out of Washington will be upbeat and positive. Government economists who even dare to suggest that the federal budget is out of control may find themselves buried in the inner sanctum of Washington, or teaching Economics 101 at a community college somewhere.

I realize that I sound like a skeptic, and I openly admit that I am. But to be fair there are some honest politicians who have attempted to expose the truth and will continue to do so. Just look for those labeled "anti-progressive" and listen to them. If you would like a current list of those considered to be the most fiscally sound thinkers, you can write to the National Taxpayers' Union, 325 Pennsylvania Ave SE, Washington DC 20003.

It is easy enough to find fault with a system like our federal bureaucracy because the abuses are visible for all to see. The question all Americans have to ask is, "What can be done about it?"

If there is nothing that can be done to change the situation, then all I will accomplish through this book is to depress some, disturb some others, and stir up a temporary flurry of activity.

I believe there is a great deal that can be done if God's people will wake up *now*. But if you get duped by the very voices I have warned against, they will convince you that this book, and all others like it, are just the distorted view of an alarmist, meant to promote some hidden agenda. This I promise you! I have no agenda other than to alert God's people to the looming crisis.

I absolutely believe what I have tried to convey to you. Obviously that does not necessarily mean I am correct; you'll have to evaluate that for yourself. But the statistics presented are easily verifiable. I have provided the sources in Appendix B. I encourage any skeptic to do the research necessary to satisfy yourself. If that doesn't convince you, then you cannot be convinced.

Perhaps some of my regular Christian readers are thinking, *Where does God fit into all this? Aren't we to trust in His provision?* Absolutely. Some of you may have been wondering why I used so few references to the only written source of absolute wisdom—God's Word—thus far. That was not an oversight. It was a deliberate decision on my part.

The information I have presented is both historical data and my personal interpretation of future events. I am not a prophet of God (that I am aware of). I have a real concern that those reading this book will not link an economic forecast with scriptural doctrine. Obviously God is in control of our economy. This nation has been blessed because, traditionally, we have taken a strong stand for the Lord. Whether or not God will continue to bless us in the future, only He knows. Our responsibility is to obey for the sake of obedience—not profit.

Just as I believe our material wealth is a by-product of observing God's commandments and following His directions, so I believe the present state of our economy is an indication of violating basic biblical principles provided in the Bible.

In Deuteronomy 28:12-13 God makes His people a promise: *"The Lord will open for you His good storehouse, the heavens, to give rain to your land in its season and to bless all the work of your hand; and you shall lend to many nations, but you shall not borrow. And the Lord shall make you the head and not the tail, and you only shall be above, and you shall not be underneath, if you will listen to the commandments of the Lord your God, which I charge you today, to observe them carefully."*

Then in Deuteronomy 28:43-45 another sobering promise is made: *"The alien who is among you shall rise above you higher and higher, but you shall go down lower and lower. He shall lend to you, but you shall not lend to him; he shall be the head, and you shall be the tail. So all these curses shall come on you and pursue you and overtake you until you are destroyed, because you would not obey the Lord your God by keeping His commandments and His statutes which He commanded you."*

Take an objective look at our economy today and see for yourself if these passages describe where we are. I pray that we can turn this economy around and save our children and grandchildren from the scourges of depression and hyperinflation. If we can, there is no time to waste.

14

WHAT CAN YOU DO?

As I have been writing, I've been thinking about what advice to give to you. The quandary I always have with giving advice is whether or not I'm willing to accept my own advice and actually do something different as a result. In all honesty, I have to admit that as I've reread this work, I have been startled by some of the statistics presented. What you are reading is a condensed version of a large volume of statistics my researcher and I accumulated over a long period of time. When I saw them all in one place I wasn't prepared for the impact it had on me. We are headed for an economic earthquake disaster of unparalleled magnitude, and it is difficult to see anything that can be done to avert it at this time.

The one certainty is that God is still in control no matter what happens. I continually remind myself that the Lord said not even a sparrow falls to the ground without His knowledge. That really is comforting, even if you happen to be that sparrow.

However, knowing that God is in control does not remove our responsibility to do everything possible to change what is happening or to prepare ourselves for some difficult times. As Proverbs 16:9 says, *"The mind of man plans his way, but the Lord directs his steps."*

The theme of a popular song a few years ago was "I didn't promise you a rose garden." The same theme can be applied to God's people in this world. Perhaps it is His will that we suffer some hard times. There is nothing that will bring the saved or unsaved to their knees like seeing their economic foundations shattered.

Most Christians in America are as much a part of the problem as anyone else.

I truly believe the decade ahead of us will provide the greatest opportunity to witness of any since the first century. We have the means to reach everyone who will listen through the electronic media; we have the trained people who can touch every level of society; and we will have the opportunity when the whole world seems to be in chaos.

The logical question that needs to be asked is, "Will Christians be a part of the solution . . . or a part of the problem?" As of this minute I would say that most Christians in America are as much a part of the problem as anyone else. There is basically no difference in how the average Christian handles his or her finances compared to the average non-Christian.

Too often Christians think that because they *are* Christians God is obligated to keep them from all harm. There are two basic flaws in that mentality.

First, a great many Christians are violating basic biblical principles in the areas of personal and business finances. God is under no obligation to bail them out of situations He has specifically warned them against in the first place. That doesn't mean that He won't. God is long-suffering when it comes to our disobedience. But it may also mean that when the Scripture gives us ample warnings we are to obey or suffer the consequences. As Proverbs 1:32-33 says, *"For the waywardness of the naive shall kill them, and the complacency of fools shall destroy them. But he who listens to me shall live securely, and shall be at ease from the dread of evil."*

Second, it may well be God's plan to allow His people, or at least some of them, to suffer along with the unbelievers. We are to witness to those around us that God is sufficient in *all* things. If Christians were removed from every problem that befalls this society, we certainly would attract a large following, but for the wrong reasons. God desires followers who will serve Him regardless of the costs. Adversity seems to strengthen us, whereas prosperity tends to weaken us. As the prophet said in Proverbs 30:8-9, *"Keep deception and lies far from me, give me neither poverty nor riches; feed me with the food that is my portion, lest I be full and deny Thee and say, 'Who is the Lord?' or lest I be in want and steal, and profane the name of my God."*

The temptations in poverty are more black and white than they are in riches. In poverty the choice is usually between being honest or dishonest. In riches we can drift away from God without even realizing it.

God often will allow His disciples (followers) to suffer adversity for the benefit of His work. You only need to look at the lives of His own apostles to verify this.

What it really boils down to is this:

1. Many Christians will suffer needlessly because of their own foolish decisions and failure to plan properly, based on God's Word.

2. Others will suffer through no fault of their own simply because God wants to use them as examples of steadfastness in the face of adversity.

3. There will be some Christians who will experience God's supernatural provision—mentally, financially, physically, and spiritually.

If I have a choice, I'll choose the last group, thank you very much. But since the choice is God's, not ours, the best you and I can do is ensure that we don't inhibit God's help because of our own foolish decisions.

Psalm 50, verses 14 and 15 are some of my most cherished Scriptures. *"Offer to God a sacrifice of thanksgiving, and pay your vows to the Most High; and call upon Me in the day of trouble; I shall rescue you, and you will honor Me."*

In these passages we are given a marvelous promise: that God will come and rescue us in our "day of trouble." I have experienced this firsthand many times. It is wonderful to stand back and see God's provision when there seems to be no human way to resolve a situation. However, if you will read those verses carefully, you will find that there are some prerequisites that must first be met.

The certainty is that without sacrifice there can be no rewards.

We are told in verse 14 to offer a sacrifice of "thanksgiving" to God. The term "sacrifice" means to surrender something we have our hearts set on (literally to give up a desire). For me at least, this has always meant the right to make my own decisions. Once I made the decision to invite Christ into my life, I gave up the right to make my own decisions. As long as I practice this principle diligently, the Lord can bless me. The instant I stop doing this, the Lord is constrained by His own Word from coming to my rescue.

Obviously there are many other areas of our lives that also must be in compliance with God's Word, but for me personally this represents the greatest challenge. For others it may be surrendering the "perfect" home or the right car or giving up a retirement plan or some other desire. The certainty is that without sacrifice there can be no rewards. That was true for Abraham, just as it is true for us today.

The second prerequisite for receiving God's help is to "pay our vows." A vow is a promise made to the Lord. Every person who has been saved into God's kingdom has made some fundamental vows that must be kept if God is to bless and protect them.

The apostle Paul said in Romans 10:9, *"If you confess with your mouth Jesus as Lord, and believe in your heart that God raised Him from the dead, you shall be saved."*

These are the two absolute vows made by *everyone* who has accepted Jesus Christ as Savior. The first is to confess Jesus as Lord. To confess Jesus as Lord with your mouth means to "agree" with God that His Son is our omnipotent authority. The term *omnipotent* means "absolute and without challenge."

If Christ is the total and absolute authority in our lives, we will obey His teachings. The Lord said in Luke 6:46, *"Why do you call Me 'Lord, Lord,' and do not do what I say?"* It cannot be said any clearer. If we call Christ Lord, we must also obey Him. The way we handle our finances is one of the clearest indicators of whether or not we are obedient to the Lord. In Matthew 7:21 Jesus said, *"Not everyone who says to Me, 'Lord, Lord,' will enter the kingdom of heaven; but he who does the will of My Father who is in heaven."*

Our second promise or vow is to "believe in our hearts" that Christ is risen from the dead. I don't know what this means to you, but to me it means that I must live my life in such a manner that Christ working through me can witness to others that He is still alive.

If my life (or yours) is lived in a manner that never reflects any supernatural circumstances, there is virtually no witness for Christ's resurrection.

There are many non-Christians who are nice, philanthropic people. Unfortunately many of them actually live a better lifestyle than many of those who claim to be Christians. But their lives reflect none of the supernatural that was so common in the Lord's day. They are basically nice people who help to ease a lot of misery on this earth, but they do nothing to ease the greater misery the vast majority will suffer for eternity.

Our lives are to reflect something greater: Jesus Christ. If we do, He has committed Himself to our rescue because then *He* will receive the glory, not us. There is an old cliché that I like to use when describing God's rescue: "never late, rarely early."

I have offered this brief review of financial principles simply to emphasize what God's Word teaches: that God will intercede on our behalf if we will allow Him to. But we can block His help by our own stubborn disobedience and disregard of His Word.

Obviously anyone wants God's help in times of trial; often there is no other place to turn. But the time to secure His help in this coming economic earthquake is right now, through obedience to His teachings and personal leading.

Only the Lord knows the future, and only the Lord has control over the future. However, by observing His principles we can make our future a whole lot less vexing. God allows us to be a part of His decision-making process. His Word teaches that we are to be a part of His plan, not just an observer of it.

"The mind of man plans his way, but the Lord directs his steps" (Proverbs 16:9).

There are some things everyone can do to prepare for the economic earthquake that is coming. These do not include buying guns, gold, dehydrated foods, and a cabin in the north woods, as some suggest. God did not raise up an army to have us cut and run every time things get rough.

The one nonvariable is this: what you own belongs to you and not a lender.

When times were difficult for the believers in Jerusalem, God already had planned for their needs through diligent converts who were debt-free and able to share with others (see Acts 4:34-35). Remember that by standing together we can meet every need and still have an abundance left over. But God's plan involves disciplined people who will read the signs and then act in accordance.

GET OUT OF DEBT

In 1989 I wrote a book entitled *Debt-Free Living*. In it I tried to discuss all the arguments for and against borrowing in our economy, so I won't expound on that material here. However, I believe there are some pertinent points that must be made in relation to the coming crisis in our economy.

First, debt created this problem, and debt will make it far worse before we see any resolution. However, debt is not the problem. Debt is merely a symptom of indulgence. Debt has allowed the government to spend money it didn't have on projects that most Americans wouldn't have approved if they had been required to pay for them with tax dollars.

Second, there is no way to sustain debt spending for an indefinite period of time. Eventually the interest accumulation will exceed anyone's (or any country's) ability to keep the debt current.

Let me restate an absolute principle of economics: No one, government or otherwise, can spend more than he or she makes indefinitely. At some point the compounding interest will consume all the money in the world. We might disagree about *when* the end will come, but not *if*.

With so many variables in the economy, the one nonvariable is this: What you *own* belongs to *you* and not to a lender. There are many people who could be debt-free just by moving funds from one investment to another, such as withdrawing funds from a retirement account to pay off their home mortgage. The reason most don't is that someone has convinced them it makes more sense to pay the interest and save the taxes.

Many unfortunate people have discovered that what seems to make sense in a stable economy becomes nonsensical in a volatile economy. I have already demonstrated that paying interest makes no sense. Unless you're in a 101 percent tax bracket, you lose more interest than you gain in tax refund.

For those who are at least twenty years from retirement, it makes economic sense to concentrate on debt retirement before saving for retirement. This is true even though the retirement funds are tax deferred, or even if the funds must be removed from an existing retirement plan.

Currently, if you take an early withdrawal on a retirement account, you will have to pay additional taxes and a penalty for early withdrawal (for those under the age of 59½). Even so, it still makes economic sense to take the penalty and pay the taxes just to know your home is debt-free. If you can't pay your real estate taxes in a bad economy, you can lose your home in three years (in most states). However, if you can't pay the mortgage payments, you can lose it in three months.

You need to look at every loan you get from this point on to determine what the contingent liabilities are. If you are obligated beyond the assigned collateral, don't borrow! If you already have loans that put you in surety, do everything possible (within reason) to retire the outstanding loans and avoid any future surety.

> ## *It is in the interest of those who rent money to keep the majority of people borrowing.*

Depending on your situation, it may not make good economic sense to sell assets or strip a retirement plan to pay off loans. But set a goal to be debt-free as soon as possible. Don't change your mind just because the short-term economy is looking better. Read the indicators and believe that our economy has some problems that cannot (or will not) be resolved.

If the economy fails before the end of this decade, there will be some people who cannot get totally debt-free. But if I am off by even a few years, and that's entirely possible, virtually anyone who desires to can become debt-free. There is no better time to begin than right now, and it starts with an attitude adjustment.

This adjustment is to make up your mind that God's Word governs your decisions, not someone else's idea of financial logic. It is in the interest of those who rent money to keep the majority of people borrowing. God's Word says that a wise man looks ahead to see if there is a problem coming and tries to avoid it. Only a naive person proceeds without caution (my paraphrase of Proverbs 27:12).

RETIREMENT PLANNING

At the risk of sounding radical, I'm going to suggest that if you are at least twenty years away from retirement you put aside your retirement goals for at least five years and concentrate on the more immediate needs, such as retiring your debts first. This may sound like a restatement of what I just discussed, and it is. But it makes economic as well as biblical sense to get totally out of debt before starting a retirement plan, especially looking ahead to some of the problems we are facing.

If you weigh the alternatives of either starting a retirement plan while paying off your home or using the retirement funds to pay your home off early and then starting the retirement plan, there is no contest. Assuming you have at least twenty years before retirement, you will do much better financially by paying off the mortgage first. It's the simple concept of compounding interest working for you rather than against you. For those who have never considered this, the chart on the following page, borrowed from a book I wrote, will verify it for you.

The example I used was a 35-year old man who plans to retire at age 65. He can save $100 in a retirement account for 30 years, while paying off his home mortgage ($100,000 at 10 percent), or he can use his extra $100 a month to prepay his mortgage and, then, start his retirement account.

Plan A shows him paying the mortgage while paying into the retirement account.

Plan B shows him paying off the mortgage, then starting the retirement account. The savings in the retirement account are compounded at 6 percent annually.

If you are within ten years of retirement, or are retired already, I would suggest some radical changes in your perspective.

For those with sizeable assets ($250,000 or more) I suggest that you follow Solomon's advice and diversify as rapidly as the economy will allow. *"Divide your portion to seven, or even to eight, for you do not know what misfortune may occur on the earth"* (Ecclesiastes 11:2).

Plan A	Plan B
$100,000 mortgage at 10% for 30 yrs. = $315,918	$100,000 mortgage at 10% for 30 yrs. plus $100 per month additional principal payment. A savings of $90,104 is realized as home is paid off in 19.3 years. = $225,814
$100 per month invested in retirement account at 6% for 30 yrs. = $101,054 (approx.)	
NET RESULT: 1. Home paid off (age 65) 2. $101,054 in savings at age 65.	After home is paid off, equivalent payments (mortgage amount plus $100) are invested in a retirement account at 6% for 10.7 years. = $178,395
	NET RESULT: 1. Home paid off (age 54) 2. $178,395 in savings at age 65.

You need to look at investing in some assets outside the United States through quality mutual funds and other instruments that have sound track records. The certainty is that the whole world's economy will not fail. Some countries will benefit while others will suffer. The difficulty is in determining which will benefit and which will not. The best "hedge" is to diversify as much as possible—not only in different areas of the economy, but also in different areas of the world. For instance, don't keep all of your assets in California real estate, even if it has always done well for you. We have not had a major economic tremor in the last fifty years, much less an economic earthquake.

The one caution I would give: Don't be panicked into making foolish investments by following the advice of those who profit from fear. More often than not these are the "gold bugs." They would have everyone place a large amount of their assets in gold or silver as protection against the big collapse.

I might put a lot more confidence in their suggestions if someone other than gold salespeople would substantiate their confidence in precious metals. There is no doubt that our economy would be better off today if we had remained on the gold standard. But we have been divorced from it for more than fifty years now. In my opinion, neither the United States nor any other major economic power will return to the gold standard in our lifetimes. To do so would require that gold be revalued to approximately $64,000 an ounce. It is far more likely that we will evolve into a totally cash-less economy as a result of the coming crisis, not one based on precious metals.

If your assets are invested too narrowly, your risk is multiplied.

For those with lesser assets and less flexibility with their retirement assets I would suggest two things: First, seek some alternative vocational training during the interval between the next upswing in the economy and the earthquake that appears to be coming. Any investment can be lost, no matter how secure it appears at present. But vocational skills will last for as long as you live and will be marketable regardless of the economy.

It is important to understand that not everyone will be mired down economically in a depression (or even in hyperinflation). Many people will actually prosper during this period because they have the resources to take advantage of the opportunities presented. This group will have the assets to pay for the services they need. So take a course in plumbing, electricity, carpentry, cosmetology, computer science, dental hygiene, or anything else that is marketable. Determine what your basic aptitudes are, and exploit them to the highest degree possible. If you can become highly proficient at any one thing, you rarely will be without a source of income.

The second suggestion is to diversify, even with limited assets. You may not be able to buy land in Poland or Yugoslavia, but you can invest in a good international mutual fund. If your assets are invested too narrowly, your risk is multiplied. Remember that the goal is not necessarily to maximize your return as much as it is to minimize your losses.

If you are retired, out of debt, and have some surplus money, in a deflationary economy your dollars will stretch farther. But if you're retired, living on a fixed income with limited assets, and hit a hyperinflationary cycle, your life savings can be consumed in a startlingly short amount of time. So it is important not to get stuck in a no-risk mentality about investing. Treasury bonds may be great in a stable or deflationary economy because they are virtually risk free. But if you believe any of the suppositions I have presented on hyperinflation might come true, you would do well to place some of your retirement assets in investments such as growth mutual funds and international funds. They won't do well during a deflationary cycle, but they will keep pace with the economy in an inflationary period.

We have allowed the political process to create a new caste system.

What happens if the government decides to absorb your retirement funds into the Social Security system? Then you simply say that you have done the best you can with what you had and go back to work again. In the meantime I would not put all my surplus into a retirement account, even if I could. In the highest tax bracket you pay about 40 percent of your earnings in federal income taxes (at present). The after-tax surplus can be invested in tax-deferred investments, such as annuities totally outside the retirement system. Based on the past actions of our government, I believe it is worth paying the taxes and controlling at least some of your savings.

One additional thing you can do is write and call your elected officials to get their official positions on the theft of funds from the Social Security Trust. If they won't take a public stand against this, make it a campaign issue during the next election. You would be amazed how agreeable many politicians are during an election period. The greatest asset we have as voters is public awareness.

GET INVOLVED

I am amazed how few people ever get involved in the political process. They have been brainwashed into believing that their voices don't really count; believe me, they do.

I had a senator tell me that as few as 200 calls or letters for or against a particular bill will often sway his vote. He also added that many of his colleagues have voiced the same comment.

We have surrendered control of our finances to a group of people ignorant in basic economics.

We have allowed the political process to create a new caste system, with our elected officials serving like a collective monarchy. They pass laws restricting the rights and freedoms for the majority of Americans, while exempting themselves from the process.

Many voters probably don't know that the Congress has exempted itself from all the civil rights and anti-discrimination laws passed. They have exempted themselves from our retirement system, our school system (for their own children), and even the normal day-care system.

It is a fact that those who vote to expand the rights of criminals and restrict the rights of the victims are themselves afraid to walk the streets of our nation's capital. The days when Harry Truman could walk the streets with little more than a token force of secret service men are over. Today the president needs an armored car and a bullet-proof vest.

The same political system that allows taxpayers' funds to be spent for a study of why bees can fly ($378,000), free playing cards for Air Force II ($52,000), anti-Christian art ($480,000), and an analysis on Hawaiian sea turtles ($250,000), also allows for our tax dollars to be poured down another ten thousand "rat holes."

Why should we think that our governmental leaders would suddenly get conservative when it comes to running our nation's economy? We have surrendered control of our finances to a group of people ignorant in basic economics. It is time that the average American wakes up and realizes that a housewife who has learned to live on an average income is eminently more qualified to make economic decisions than the average politician.

This is not a philosophical or even a political issue. It is our future we're discussing, and if we don't make some dramatic changes, it is just a matter of time before the economy fails. Keep in mind that the people who are trying to convince us that an economic crisis will not occur are the same ones who spend $500 for hammers that are commercially available for $12, buy 20 cent bolts for $60, spend $40 billion a year in taxpayers' funds not to grow food, and increase the welfare rolls from 6 million to 25 million people while spending $3.5 trillion to accomplish this remarkable task.

The list of abuses could go on and on. The point is, the next time you think that you may not be qualified to counsel the politicians on how the economy should be run, consider whether or not you would pay annual bonuses to the post office administrators who operate the postal system in the red each and every year.

If you balance your checkbook every month you're probably better qualified economically than the majority of our budget directors. I have often believed that the nation's budget directors should be required to demonstrate that they live on a budget themselves. But perhaps that's too simplistic for Washington.

If you don't want your children and grandchildren to live in a third-rate country with fewer jobs and total dependency on foreign goods and money, you *need* to get involved.

As Harry Figgie accurately stated, "This is not a Republican or a Democratic problem. It is an American problem."

I will admit that I am a radical when it comes to this issue. I watch the economy month in, month out, and I see the steady decline in competitiveness. I see politicians chiding the "wealthy" and then voting salaries for themselves that place them in the top 5 percent of incomes in America. I see honest, small business people struggling to survive under the heavy burden of taxes, insurance, and foreign competition. Our political system makes us especially vulnerable to outside competition because our government gives benefits to our competitors while penalizing American companies. It would seem the basic philosophy of our government is to help your enemies and hurt your friends. The Japanese, for instance, consider their entrepreneurs a national resource and do everything possible to preserve and protect them—even creating special legislation in order to make them more competitive.

We do the exact opposite. President Calvin Coolidge once said, "The chief business of American people is business." Our present herd of politicians no longer accept that doctrine. Their philosophy is "The business of America is politics." Unfortunately they have been quite successful in convincing Americans that the economy runs to serve the political system.

This constant and growing drain on our resources strips the business community of the vital capital needed to create more jobs and compete with countries that take our innovations and sell them back to us.

Here are a few specific suggestions you can use when contacting your senators and members of Congress.

1. Demand that the Congress and the president abide by the Gramm-Rudman Act and balance the national budget.

I would further demand that *all* spending programs be included in the law—no exceptions. Until and unless all spending is included "on-budget," the law will not work. It is very much like the wage and price controls we discussed earlier; the exceptions quickly become the norm.

What happens in the Washington political system is a process called "trade offs." In this process those who want something trade a favor for a favor. The result is usually legislation that is good for their district but bad for the country. The only way to avoid this (if at all) is to require all programs to be cut by the same percentage and to allow line-item vetoes so that so-called pork barrel spending is not attached to nonrelated legislation.

2. Keep track of how the politicians in your area vote on spending bills.

Both Citizens Against Government Waste and the National Taxpayers Union (see Appendix A) watch this area carefully and publish a quarterly report. I can assure you that if you come to an election meeting armed with specific facts about how your representatives voted to use taxpayers' money, they will think about the bills they back the next time they vote in Washington.

3. Every chance you get, challenge the mentality that all business people and the profits they generate are somehow inherently evil. That is total nonsense and merely a method of "scapegoating."

Instead, begin to prompt your elected officials to use the system to promote more competitive enterprises. I personally would like to see the government allow tax-free return on investments made to businesses that compete directly with foreign imports.

In reality we would be losing very few tax dollars since these are industries where we are no longer competitive anyway. And for every tax dollar lost, it has been shown that we would gain nearly $1,000 in taxable revenue.

Such an idea would not set well with the liberals who point their fingers at the "greedy" businesspeople, but it will set very well with the Americans who find new jobs opening up.

It is a national disgrace that Americans invented the multivalve car engine, video recorders, color televisions, digital electronics, computer-controlled machines, and so on, but are no longer competitive in the manufacturing stage in any of these industries.

It is *not* that the Asians work harder. They simply work smarter. Their politicians look upon them as partners, not as criminals.

4. Check out the curriculum being taught in your local schools and see if it is anti-free-market. It would shock most Americans to realize that a great deal of the economic information being fed their children in elementary schools, high schools, and especially state universities is blatantly socialistic, if not openly communistic.

The only place that communism still seems to flourish is in the American classroom. It is often labeled "socialism" but, in reality, it is the same doctrine that was taught in the Soviet Union prior to the communism collapse: Government is the protector of the downtrodden; capitalism is inherently evil; people deserve decent incomes, regardless of their desire to work or not; and last, the government is a better purveyor of the nation's resources than the wage earners are.

If you don't believe this is what is being taught to your children, write and ask for a copy of the National Education Association's annual resolutions (available from Eagle Forum, Box 618, Alton, IL 62002. Or better yet, just check out a copy of your child's civics book and read it.

5. *Last, and most important, we as Christians must return to our foundation: Jesus Christ. It is clear that we are not battling against flesh and blood but against principalities and powers. How else can anyone explain what is happening? Rational, intelligent people are destroying the very system that has yielded so much, and yet they don't see it.*

A dear friend of mine once said about Christianity, "If it doesn't work for you, please don't export it." I agree with that sentiment totally. If we can't get our own finances under control and learn to live on what we make, how can we demand that the government do so?

If we continue to take handouts from the government, how can we speak out against government waste? To take a stand against waste means that God's people also must refuse to take FHA or VA loans. Christian farmers need to say, "Thanks, but no thanks, Uncle." Churches need to take care of their own poor, rather than expecting welfare or Medicaid to do so.

In short, it means "walking our talk." James said in his letter: *"But prove yourselves doers of the word, and not merely hearers who delude themselves"* (James 1:22).

I believe I have done what the Lord asked of me: I have warned you. If I am wrong and you do all the things I have suggested, the worst that can happen is that you will be out of debt and more involved with our political system.

If I am right and you do nothing, you'll end up losing everything you own and be totally dependent on the very system that created the mess we are facing. Keep in mind that God has everything under control. You can do your part by giving sacrificially to the Lord's work; if you do, you cannot lose. *"Because of the proof given by this ministry they will glorify God for your obedience to your confession of the gospel of Christ, and for the liberality of your contribution to them and to all"* (2 Corinthians 9:13).

Just as the day of the Lord will come as a thief in the night, so an economic collapse will come in the midst of what appears to be economic prosperity. The very debt that creates the prosperity ultimately destroys it.

If you truly surrender your finances to God, you will experience His faithfulness. I pray the Lord will give you the wisdom to do as He directs you.

Note: This completes Part I of this book which, with the exception of updates, was published in 1991. Part II, which is all new material, follows.

PART 2

15

THE IMPACT OF THE 1993 TAX BILL

In spite of conclusive historical evidence that lowering taxes *stimulates* a stagnant economy and raising taxes *depresses* it, in the early stages of his administration President Clinton sponsored the biggest single tax increase since World War II.

One might wonder why any president would do such a thing, especially since his election was based on a platform of reducing the federal deficit and restarting our faltering economy.

In the first place, government statistics conclusively show that the economy was improving steadily before Bill Clinton was elected. Whether the press purposely suppressed the facts to hurt George Bush, you'll have to decide for yourself. It seems clear enough that the facts were suppressed and, in fact, George Bush did lose the election.

An argument can be made that the tax increase was a part of President Clinton's promise to reduce the deficits. After all, his primary justification for the new tax bill was that, although approximately $256 billion in new taxes would be raised, this was absolutely necessary in order to bring the deficits down.

Remember, candidate Clinton promised that for every dollar of new taxes raised at least $3 of government spending would be cut. Apparently, what he really meant was that for every dollar of new taxes raised $3 of *proposed* spending would be cut.[1]

In the final analysis, even if all of the spending cuts built into the 1993 Omnibus Budget Reconciliation Act are made, the overall federal debt still will rise by more than $1 trillion by the end of this president's first term in office. So if everything the new tax bill promises comes true (highly unlikely), the government will take $250 billion in taxes out of the private sector economy, to be disbursed by Washington, and also add an additional $1 trillion in new debt.

If my math serves me correctly, Bill Clinton has absolutely committed to spend an additional $1.3 trillion, even with his "budget cuts." Lumped in with former President Bush's $170 billion tax increase, we're going to have another $1.5 trillion siphoned off the economy. At a time when the government should be reducing spending, it's doing just the opposite.

Will there be some economic repercussions as a result of sending an additional $1.5 trillion through the labyrinth of Washington? Well, if not, I suggest that the government simply do away with all personal and corporate income taxes and borrow all the operating funds for the federal government.

President Clinton would have done well to heed some of the advice given by his boyhood hero, President John F. Kennedy.

In 1962 President Kennedy gave a speech before the Economic Club of New York, where he outlined his plan for economic recovery. The following is an excerpt from that speech.

The most direct and significant kind of federal action aiding economic growth is to make possible an increase in private consumption and investment demand—to cut the fetters which hold back private spending. . . .

The . . . best means of strengthening demand among consumers and business is to reduce the burden on private income and the deterrents to private initiative that are imposed by our present tax system—and this administration [has] pledged itself . . . to an across-the-board, top-to-bottom cut in personal and corporate income taxes to be enacted and become effective in 1963. . . .

In short, to increase demand and lift the economy, the federal government's most useful role is not to rush into a program of excessive increases in public expenditures, but to expand the incentives and opportunities for private expenditures. . . .

The purpose of cutting taxes . . . is not to incur a budget deficit, but to achieve [a] more prosperous, expanding economy which can bring a budget surplus.

The economic platform adopted by Kennedy was not actually of his own design. Kennedy modeled his plan on the economic revitalization policies of West German Chancellor Konrad Adenauer.

It is a historical fact that actual revenues rarely, if ever, reach the expectations of those who persist in increasing taxes.

At that time the West Germans had an economy that was the envy of the free world. Their unemployment rate was essentially zero, inflation was low, and German products were in great demand. Socialism had yet to raise its ugly head, and the German workers were among the most productive in the world. West Germany was on a roll.

Adenauer believed that higher taxes result in slower economic growth, which results in lower government revenues.

Such a relationship is demonstrated clearly in the graphs. The first shows that whether taxes are high or low, the government nets about the same percentage of Gross Domestic Product (GDP).

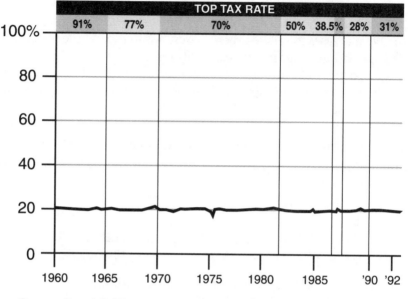

Federal Government Receipts
As Percentage of Gross Domestic Product

Source: Crandall, Pierce

The logical reason for this apparent phenomenon is that GDP growth slows with a tax increase. The principle presented is one commonly taught in Economics 101: Taking a small portion of a large pie is better than a larger portion of a much smaller pie. It is a historical fact that actual revenues rarely, if ever, reach the expectations of those who persist in increasing taxes. Not only does the economy slump, the people who would pay the higher taxes simply make adjustments to avoid paying them. This is especially true of higher income people who have the resources to either shift their investments or adjust their productivity.[2]

The 1986 Tax Reform Act raised the capital gains tax rate from 20 percent to as much as 33 percent. By 1991 the tax increase was supposed to bring in $285 billion in capital gains tax. Instead, the 1991 figure was only $108 billion. One study estimated that if the tax rate had been left at 20 percent, revenue would have been $166 billion higher. In other words, the lower tax rate would have brought in $58 billion more in revenue![3]

The Capital Gains Tax
(Rates and Revenues)

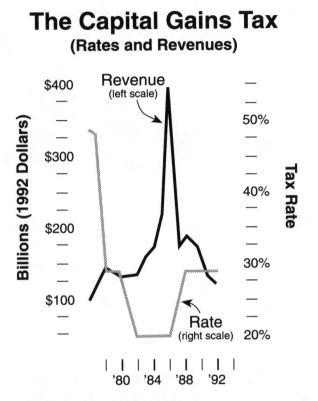

Source: Internal Revenue Service

Even with all of this evidence, politicians persist in thinking that they can *tax* their way out of the problems they create. If that were so, socialism would be the dominant economic force in the world today. After all, socialism is merely a redistribution of wealth through taxation.

Now, let's look at the spending side of the 1993 tax bill. As the facts show, nearly 80 percent of all Clinton's proposed spending reductions are scheduled to take effect after 1995.

Scheduled Spending Cuts

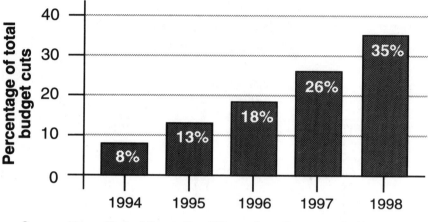

Source: House Budget Committee (Figures have been rounded.)

The probability of this ever happening can be demonstrated by the Gramm-Rudman Act, which established mandatory budget cuts in order to balance the federal budget by 1991. Decide for yourself how effective future budget cuts are in controlling Washington's appetite for spending money.

Deficit Growth Under Gramm-Rudman Acts

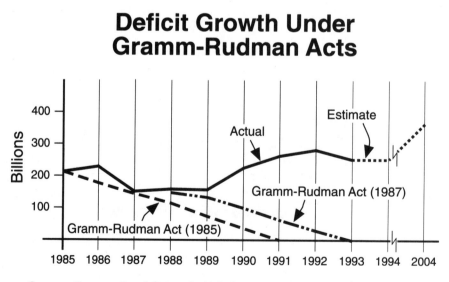

Source: Congressional Quarterly, U.S. Department of the Treasury, and Congressional Budget Office

We certainly have come a long way from the debate that took place on the floor of the House in 1834, when Congressman Davey Crockett stood up and scolded his colleagues for even suggesting that the government should take public monies to support a war veteran's widow. He knew the warning George Washington, Thomas Jefferson, James Madison, Benjamin Franklin, and others had given to succeeding generations: To open the public treasuries to private needs, no matter how just, would ultimately lead to the bankruptcy of the republic.

I'm sure the examples of Rome and Greece still lingered in the minds of the founding fathers. Once those governments instituted public support to appease the masses, it was only a matter of time until their economies failed.

When income taxes were authorized by the 16th amendment to the Constitution, the supporters of this amendment had no concept of what would evolve. Heated debates on the House floor centered around establishing specific limits on how much Americans could be taxed. Clearly, the Constitution prohibited the unequal taxation of any one citizen over another.

The principle was well established: The power to tax involves the power to destroy. Once any government has the ability to single out one class or group for special tax rates, it can reward or punish them. The danger of this happening was the logic behind the founders limiting government revenues to only sales, excise taxes, or other tariffs. This all changed with the adoption of the 16th amendment, which provided for unequal taxation based on incomes.

It wasn't difficult to sell the general public on the concept of an income tax on the "wealthy" of the early twentieth century (sound familiar?). After all, it didn't seem fair that a few people like Henry Ford, J. Paul Getty, or John D. Rockefeller should be allowed to make so much money and contribute so little to the "general welfare" of the country.

What the voters and politicians both failed to grasp was that entrepreneurs, in the process of acquiring wealth, do contribute to the general welfare. There is no question that in the early days of the industrial revolution in America many industrialists underpaid and overworked their employees. But as production grew and labor became scarce, the tables turned, and labor was able to negotiate higher wages and better working conditions.

Men like Henry Ford were the risk takers who were confident enough in their own abilities to launch new ideas. Certainly they got wealthy, maybe even "filthy rich," but they reinvested much of it into the economy; and others also were made rich. This is not possible without available investment capital. Government does not create new capital; it consumes it.

> *The reason I dedicated space to this particular tax increase is because it represents the basic philosophy of the Clinton administration: bigger government.*

In 1914 the first income tax authorized under the 16th amendment levied a one percent tax on incomes above $3,000 a year ($40,000 in '93 dollars), with a surtax of up to 6 percent on incomes above $500,000. By 1917 the tax rates were 7 percent to 77 percent, and the minimum taxable wage was $1,000. So much for political promises, then and now.[4]

So another income tax increase is not the most significant event of the history of Washington, D.C. There have been many in the past and, without a doubt, there will be many more to come. The reason I dedicated space to this particular tax increase is because it represents the basic philosophy of the Clinton administration: bigger government.

It has been said that President Clinton is just another tax-and-spend Democrat. That is not entirely true. He is an absolute believer in the ability of government to solve almost any problem, given enough money to do so.

Clinton was born in a small, semi-rural state but educated in the "Great Society" mentality. In terms of social policy, Mrs. Clinton was noted as a radical thinker even while she was in college.

Both of the Clintons' pre-Washington careers reflect a determination to put government in charge of as much of our lives as possible. We should not be surprised to find that their agenda hasn't changed simply because they wield more authority now. In fact, we should expect the agenda to escalate proportionally to the new power they have at their disposal.

Understanding this philosophy is essential to understanding the future direction of our economy. When I finished *The Coming Economic Earthquake* in 1991, I said there was little that any president could do to salvage our economy. The debt is too large, the deficits too deep, and the politicians too timid (with some notable exceptions) to do what is necessary.

What I did not say was how much damage a liberal president could do with a liberal Congress to support his programs. We will most certainly know the answer to that question between now and 1996.

At this juncture I am tempted to launch into a discussion of the Clintons' social programs, which range from active recruitment of homosexuals in policy-making positions, to avowed Socialists planning the economic policies of our nation, to pro-abortionists heading the national health care industry; but I will not do that.

From the ashes of our economy may come a new form of economics. In that economy the government will take control.

I trust that others within the Christian community will address the social issues, which do not bode well for our Christian values under the Clinton administration. Certainly pornographers will receive more tolerance than Christians in the Clinton justice department. But since this book is meant to deal with economic issues, I will stick with that topic.

The bottom line is that we have an administration that is socialistic in economic perspective and will not hesitate to expand government control, if it helps to promote its social programs.

A good friend in Congress told me recently that he sees no real hope of correcting the problems in our economy. In fact, he reported, it would seem that the majority in Congress and the president are determined to destroy our economic system.

When I suggested that perhaps they were operating out of ignorance, this long-time congressman replied, "You don't understand; this crowd knows that real power comes only through social upheaval. They are willing to sacrifice our economy on the altar of socialism. They simply will overload this economy until it collapses. Then they will blame the greedy capitalists and promote greater socialism."

As I have considered what he said, I think there is a great deal of truth in it. From the ashes of our economy may come a new form of economics. In that economy the government will take control—even of what we can buy and sell. Perhaps it will be a totally cashless monetary system. It's really too early to tell.

If you think this scenario is farfetched, just keep your eyes and ears open as the economy really begins to unravel. See if government social programs are pegged as the root causes of our economic problems or whether the free enterprise system is blamed. Americans already are being fed a steady diet of propaganda about the heartlessness of the greedy entrepreneurs in our society.

Middle income taxpayers will probably see a reduction in allowable exemptions, which is a sure-fire method to raise revenue.

The media focus their attention on the few unscrupulous businesspeople who pillage their companies for personal gain. They *never* focus on the small entrepreneur struggling with an incomprehensible bureaucracy, excessive taxes, and a hostile business environment in Washington. The politicians talk about helping American businesses to compete; then they pass more regulations that make it virtually impossible.

Every failed society has needed scapegoats in times of trouble. In my opinion, two groups will be targeted. Christians will be condemned for their social and moral "inflexibility," and entrepreneurs will be blamed for the failing economy and resultant unemployment. Already laws like the RICO Act (Racketeering-Influenced and Corrupt Organization statute) are being applied to abortion protests.

WHO WILL PAY THE BILLS?

In spite of all the rhetoric about taxing the wealthy, there just is not enough money in that group to fund the new social programs and reduce the deficit—even slightly. Of all the million or so income tax returns filed, only about .7 percent of those who filed showed incomes of $200,000 or more.[5]

The real money is to be found in the other 99.3 percent—most of whom are average income taxpayers. It is this group that will be asked to "contribute" next.

It is almost a certainty that President Clinton will sponsor more tax increases before his term in office is over. Clearly without some attempt to rein in deficits, he will be a one-term president. Since Clinton subscribes to the higher-taxes-equal-lower-deficit theory, apparently there is no thought of lowering taxes to reduce the deficits.

It is highly probable that we will see some modified form of value-added tax; and middle income taxpayers will probably see a reduction in allowable exemptions, which is a sure-fire method to raise revenue.

Nonprofit organizations will be facing an increasingly hostile tax environment. I expect the exemption of many organizations to be challenged to the highest degree ever by any administration. The most likely challenge will be aimed at what is called disassociated income: income derived from sources other than contributions, such as day care, school tuitions, book sales, and so on.

Increasingly, the courts also are applying the concept of "benefit to the community at large" to nonprofit organizations. Those who fail this test will find their tax-exempt status being challenged. Few Christian organizations, outside of the Salvation Army and Habitat for Humanity perhaps, would meet this test.

Perhaps I have totally misread the Clinton administration and the president will convert to a free market advocate and try to get government out of health care, environmental regulation, raising taxes, and micro-managing the economy; but I don't think so. If he were going to follow the examples of John Kennedy and Ronald Reagan and lower taxes, he would have to do so quickly—to avert what appears to be a major economic downturn in late 1994 or early 1995.

If, instead, we see the administration pushing for even higher taxes and more regulation, then you will know that the scenario I have presented here is at least reasonably on target.

I would like to share one additional thought before moving on to another topic. If anyone needs examples of what not to do to our economy, they need look no further than Western Europe and the economic mess they're in today.

The Socialists might argue that the collapse of the Soviet Union and Eastern Europe was not the result of socialism because the USSR really had operated under a tyrannical dictatorship of sorts since the Bolshevik revolution. But no one can make that comment about Western Europe. Those countries are democracies conducting a socialistic economic experiment.

Almost the whole of Western Europe is experiencing a major recession that appears to have no solution. Unemployment is as high as 22 percent in some countries, and businesses are fleeing the highly regulated western economies for the unregulated eastern countries.

It is not primarily high wages that is driving out businesses and slowing their economies. Instead, it is the cost of government-mandated benefits, which often add as much as 100 percent to the cost of labor.

A survey of German companies shows that as many as 30 percent of all manufacturers are planning to relocate to the East. The German garment company, Adolf Ahlers (AG) exemplifies this problem. In 1970 the company employed 5,000 workers. Today it still employees 5,000, but only 40 now work in Germany. When asked the reason for moving most of the jobs to the East, the company president replied, "It's simple logic: The cost of doing business in Germany is too high."

With massive cutbacks in Europe and England, the Socialists there are discovering (or rediscovering) the truth about economics: If you can't make a profit, you can't stay in business; and if your company can't stay in business you won't have a job—no matter how many promises the government makes.

In Sweden, the classic example of socialistic success, reality has come home also. Since 1990, Swedish economic output has dropped 7 percent, while unemployment has risen from 3 percent to 13 percent. To help absorb the increased unemployment without sacrificing benefits, the government of Sweden doubled the national debt to nearly 13 percent of the economy's output (GDP).

The same old socialistic policies that we are now adopting in this country will eventually return any industrialized society to Third World status.

For nearly the entire decade of the eighties, Sweden was touted by American Socialists as an example of what total government management could accomplish. The Swedes provided universal health insurance, unemployment benefits almost equal to lost wages, one year paid leave for childbirth, government-subsidized child care, and 60 days a year paid leave to care for a sick child or relative. And, although the government was spending 57 percent of GDP on social programs, the unemployment rate was only 3 percent.

The way the government accomplished this "miracle" was by constantly expanding government employment to cover the loss of private sector jobs. When the source of taxes began to dry up, they started printing money to cover the shortfall. The theory was to inflate the currency to make debt repayment less painful. But when the inflation rate began to get out of hand, the government had to cut back. Suddenly, the good times were over.

In an effort to entice businesses back that have relocated elsewhere, Sweden is now trying to reduce welfare and work benefits, cut spending, and lower taxes and regulations.

What the lessons of Sweden and the rest of Europe demonstrate is that the same old socialistic policies that we are now adopting in this country will eventually return any industrialized society to Third World status.[6]

Many of our liberal politicians, with their feet firmly planted in mid air, simply refuse to learn from the mistakes of others. We seem bound and determined to prove history wrong once again.

NOTES

1. Robert W. Lee, "The Deficit Reduction Game," *New American,* 7/12/93, pp. 13-15.

2. W. Kurt Hauser, "A Constant Relationship," *The Wall Street Journal,* 8/6/93.

3. Thomas McArdle, "Can Government Afford Capital Gains Hike?" *Investor's Business Daily*, 7/22/93.

4. Nancy Shepherdson, "The First 1040," *American Heritage*, 3/89.

5. "Tax Report: A Special Summary and Forecast of Federal and State Tax Developments," *The Wall Street Journal*, 7/7/93.

6. Peter Gumbel, "Western Europe Finds That It's Pricing Itself Out of the Job Market," *The Wall Street Journal,* 12/9/93; Robert J. Samuelson, "The Swedish Disease," *Washington Post,* 12/8/93.

16
THE HEALTH SECURITY ACT

I wish we had a firm understanding of how Congress will treat President Clinton's health care plan, but it simply does not exist at this time. I have a copy of what is called the Health Security Act (catchy title!). In reality it is a convoluted assortment of the ideas dredged up by Mrs. Clinton's National Health Care Task Force.

Most of the specific proposals made in the Health Security Act (HSA) will be greatly modified as this plan makes its way through the Congress. The one concept that probably will survive is the idea that it is the government's responsibility to "fix" our health care system.

The last time our government decided to fix a national problem, it was welfare. That fix has made life in the city a living nightmare. And keep in mind, the entire welfare program is less than one-fifth the size of the health care system that President Clinton is attempting to fix.

If the concept of federally mandated health care for all Americans is accepted, it cannot be reversed. The beginning program may be modest in scope, but don't be deceived. The details will be fleshed out in the halls of Congress, one bill at a time. Politicians love to give things away, and this is the biggest plum of all.

I think back to the days before Lyndon Johnson's Great Society, when most Americans didn't believe it was the government's responsibility to feed and house the poor, provide medical coverage for the elderly, or guarantee cradle-to-grave social programs for every man, woman, and child.

"But these are worthwhile programs," some would argue. Indeed, they might be if they were administered by private institutions with no vested interests, such as getting elected. But when the government assumes the role of the "Great Provider," the mouse grows to elephantine proportions.

We were told in 1964 that every American deserved a safety net that would ensure adequate housing and food, even if they could not (or would not) work. We (compassionate Americans) listened and allowed our representatives to pass Lyndon Johnson's Economic Opportunity Act, which he told us would conquer hunger in America in 20 years, at a cost of less than $60 billion (total).

Here we are, $3.5 trillion later, and there are just as many people living below poverty level now as there were in 1964.[1]

Many Americans actually believe the same government that brought us welfare, school busing, and $500 hammers can reform, regulate, and otherwise perfect our health care system.

In addition, as a result of our strategic government planning, we have rampant crime in the inner cities, where welfare is most prevalent. Youths who have been raised without any traditional family structure now terrorize their neighborhoods. Not only is one-on-one violent crime escalating in these government-administered ghettos, but illegitimate births have soared to 80 percent, illiteracy is similar to most Third World countries, and drugs and gangs rule the streets.

Society pays far beyond the direct cost of welfare in robberies, rapes, murders, property devaluation, police, and prisons. And remember, welfare programs are designed, administered, and controlled *totally* by the government.

In the case of welfare, we have tried. And it failed. As I said earlier, there is some hope for the future because even many social liberals now see welfare as a harmful entitlement and are seeking to reform it. Obviously true reform has to come in the minds and hearts of the people involved on both sides. The real problem is a lack of spiritual values in our society, which is being reflected in the behaviors of those raised without values.

What astounds me is that many Americans actually believe the same government that brought us welfare, school busing, and $500 hammers can reform, regulate, and otherwise perfect our health care system. I recently saw a bumper sticker in Washington that said it all: If you think health care is expensive now, just wait until it's "free."

As noted earlier, the plan that President Clinton has proposed will bear faint resemblance to that which will ultimately clear the Congress. But once the process of government control of health care has begun, it will be irreversible. The very structure of more regulation and control will destroy the existing private system and make it impossible to reverse the changeover.

For instance, if the health alliances that regulate costs are installed, the majority of private insurance companies will be forced out, leaving only a few large providers. Effectively, these will become government-sponsored monopolies (more correctly, oligopolies—a market situation in which each of a few producers affects but does not control the market).

It will be next to impossible to restore the more competitive system again. Once doctors are forced out of private practice and into the alliances, it would be virtually impossible to restart these practices. Literally, we are being asked to burn our bridges.

The Roman generals often did this when invading an enemy's country. One might logically ask, "Where are the Romans today?" Many of them were left dead on the beaches.

I have to be honest and say that I don't trust the instincts of President Clinton and his wife. I'm sure they feel that if they'd been in on the beginning stages of welfare or school "reform" they could have averted some of our current problems through more government control. In truth, that does nothing more than reaffirm my concerns.

Remember the adage: Those who fail to learn from the past are doomed to repeat it. Unfortunately, we are the ones who will pay the price. Neither the Congress nor the president will be subject to the system they are designing for the rest of us.

THE EFFECTS OF THE HEALTH SECURITY ACT

Since the actual plan has not been determined as of this date, the best I can do is make an educated guess—based on what I have read and my recent conversations with members of Congress. It is important that you understand the scope and direction the Health Security Act proposes and also its potential economic impact.

I have read the president's plan as thoroughly as possible and discussed with friends in Washington what may or may not pass the Congress. I sincerely pray that the American people will rise up against the very concept of socialized medicine. But in reality, it seems certain that some form of national health care will be passed.

There are no crystal balls that foresee the future; nor am I a prophet who can predict what will come. The best I can do is equate what the government has done in the past with what seems probable for the future.

Maybe I'm being too pessimistic. Perhaps Americans will say enough is enough at the polls in 1994 and actually elect men and women to the government who will restore our Republic. But again, I have to be honest and say that I really don't believe that will happen. The older, more conservative generation is too concerned about hanging on to what they already have, and the younger generation actually believes that the government is capable of solving our problems.

The question on the minds of some three million Americans employed in the health care industry is what health care reform will do to them. To peer into the minds of those who will ultimately draft this legislation, I have relied heavily on the counsel and writings of several good friends in Washington. No doubt there will be several proposals in both the House and Senate; but, eventually one primary system (or concept) will prevail.

I will focus on the concept of Clinton's Health Security Act because discerning the details so far in advance would be fruitless. It is entirely possible that no health care legislation will be passed until after the 1994 elections. The heated debate on both sides of this issue makes most politicians very nervous. Both sides will probably throw some ideas on the table and then stand back to see how the public will react.

Very possibly, unless a clear consensus is reached before, they will use the '94 elections as a test for popular support. I'll guarantee that if you'll write about this issue to your senators and representatives in Congress, they will listen.

Most likely, the Democrats will push for some kind of health care legislation prior to the elections, since they look for their primary base of support within organized labor, minority groups, and Social Security recipients. Generally speaking, these are the people who feel they will benefit most from socialized medicine but, in my opinion, will be hurt most by socialized health care.

It is naïve to think that the federal government can operate anything more efficiently and at less cost than the private enterprise system.

Under any form of socialized health care, virtually everyone I have talked with agrees that rationing will be necessary in order to meet budget constraints; and the overall quality of health care will decline.

Right now the added costs of caring for the poor and elderly are passed along through higher insurance premiums, higher deductibles, bigger co-payments, and shifting costs to the more affluent health care users. Passing along these additional costs when taxes must be raised will not be politically popular. The probable alternative will be rationing the amount of health care provided.

When this happens, the very people who thought they would benefit the most will be among the first excluded. Undoubtedly, public sentiment will dictate that the needs of a 10-year-old with leukemia must come before a 70-year-old who needs dialysis treatment.

Today, a 70-year-old patient can get treatment through Medicare/Medicaid, private insurance, or private benevolence. Under the health care plan presented by the Clinton administration, to negotiate for care outside the plan would be a crime.[2]

Those who are more affluent still will be able to get the supplemental care they need, provided they are willing to leave the country. Undoubtedly, there will be off-shore medical clinics set up to provide critical care for those who can afford it. Medical specialists will be drawn to hospitals in the Bahamas, Caymans, Cuba, and elsewhere to practice their skills away from the confines of the Health Security Act. I'll also expect that many of our politicians will not hesitate to avail themselves of these services if they or their families need critical medical care.

ESTIMATING THE COST OF SOCIALIZED MEDICINE

The major economic issue associated with health care is the cost of operating the system. It is naïve to think that the federal government can operate anything more efficiently and at less cost than the private enterprise system. In its worst day, private enterprise is more efficient than government. Take a look at any area where they compete directly and see if that's not so.

Many municipalities are privatizing services like garbage pickup, fire prevention—even security—and realizing significant savings, as well as better quality. There are many more areas where private-versus-public service has proved its worth.

Private education delivers better quality at less cost; parcel delivery is more efficient and less costly through private carriers; even private hospitals, in general, operate more efficiently than government-owned V.A. hospitals.[3]

No doubt there are inefficiencies that can and should be corrected in the free enterprise health care business. There are too many different types of forms to fill out, depending on the insurer involved. There are too many duplicated services available at many competing hospitals. There is an abundance of price gouging when critical services are needed.

However, any and all of these can be cured without a government takeover. It can be accomplished by a simple overhaul of how services are negotiated between health providers and their patients. Simply put, people will be a lot more prudent if they are spending their own money rather than someone else's.

A study by the National Center for Policy Analysis (NCPA) pointed out that as much as 50 percent of all the increases in health care costs during the eighties and nineties can be attributed to government-sponsored health care services. How then can we realistically expect that more government control will solve the cost problem, except through rationing?

The NCPA study also pointed out that government spending now accounts for more than one-half of all health care dollars spent, and the government takes three to four dollars out of the economy for every dollar spent on health care. In other words, government can't cure the problem. It is a large part of the problem.[4]

If private insurance providers attempted to extend current health coverage and benefits to all Americans, regardless of pre-existing health conditions, as Clinton has proposed, the entire insurance industry would deplete its reserves in only a few months. Then how will the government accomplish this task while reducing the costs? Quite simply, it won't.

The costs will be disguised in the beginning and then increased, as necessary, to accomplish the real goal of national health care: government control over an additional 14 percent of our total economy.

The following chart shows the projected and actual costs of Medicare (a totally government-managed system) from its start in 1966 to 1993. Just multiply these figures by about 500 percent, and you can envision the effect of the Health Security Act.

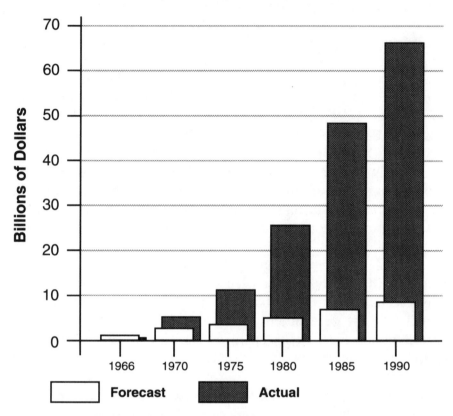

Medicare Costs

Source: Federal Hospital Insurance Trust Fund

However, the American people may never know the true cost of HSA. In typical fashion, the Clinton administration wants to keep health care spending off-budget—meaning it will not be reflected as taxes raised and money spent.

If Congress goes along with the president, it would mean that the employees' and employers' portions of health care contributions will be treated as "insurance premiums," not taxes, even though they will be mandatory, collected through payroll deductions, and the amounts will be set by the government. Unbelievable!

The politicians are going to tell us that a duck is no longer a duck—because they say it isn't. Under this non-tax category,

216

there would be no congressional control over increases in spending, and the true figures would be disguised under "off-budget appropriations."

In the meantime, employers and employees will be paying a higher premium for less health care. Obviously there will be some winners in a government health care system. Many of these will be the permanently uninsured and the uninsurable.

I personally believe it is not constitutional for the government to mandate *universal health coverage for all Americans.*

Among this group are hundreds of thousands of high-risk health cases, such as drug users, prostitutes, homosexuals, and street people. Averaging them into the total health care system cost will be expensive. People who basically accept no responsibility for their own health will make it difficult for those who do. Remember, under the proposed system, everyone will have equal access and equal care, irrespective of their lifestyles.

Let me add that I personally believe it is not constitutional for the government to *mandate* universal health coverage for all Americans. That is an authority the founders of our country never conveyed to the federal government. But in our era of reinterpreting the Constitution at whim, this probably will make little or no difference. The social reformers now running our country will accept nothing less than totally mandated coverage for everyone.

HEALTH CARE PROBLEMS

If you look at our current health care system, the flaws are obvious; they have been inviting government intervention. It's a shame that private industry didn't address these problems earlier and circumvent the reformers in government. But, it didn't.

217

The basic problems:

1. Health care costs have been escalating at a rate in excess of 300 percent of the consumer price index. Thus, many people cannot afford it.

2. Most health care insurance is tied to employment and thus can be lost if a worker is unemployed.

3. Many people are denied health insurance based on pre-existing conditions.

Because of these flaws in our health care system, it is assumed that only the government can "fix" it. The cost for doing so has been estimated to be between $40 and $150 billion per year in *additional* spending.[5]

This cost has been and will be debated as the health care bills pass through Congress. Some will say it is more; some will say it is less. No one who is reasonably intelligent will say that there won't be additional costs.

It is difficult for me to even imagine that we, as a nation, are considering such an expansive and potentially disastrous program at a time when the survival of our economy is in jeopardy. If, in fact, any form of national health care is implemented, it will be the final straw—the dagger in the heart of our economy as we know it.

There are several proposals in the works that are far saner than what is proposed by President Clinton's wife. Senators Phil Gramm and Don Nickels have submitted such a plan, along with a similar House version sponsored by Congressman Dan Burton and others.

Perhaps if enough people understand the economic risks, we will be able to exert enough pressure on the Congress to bring back some sanity. Given the past history of many of our liberal politicians, however, even that is doubtful. Probably only a changing of the "guard" will help.

I would like to address the basic issues related to our current health system "crisis." The issues are not really all that complex; we're talking about a government takeover of a $900-billion-a-year industry.

ESCALATING COSTS OF HEALTH CARE

There is no doubt that the ever-increasing costs of health care must be brought into line, because since 1980 health care costs have risen more than twice as fast as the annual consumer price index, and spending on health care is taking a growing percentage of our gross domestic product. But several undiscussed factors have contributed to much of that increase.

Are we as a people going to practice eugenics, in which doctors who are responsible to government auditors make the decisions about who is allowed to live, based on their potential benefit to society?

First, we have a lot more older Americans using our health care facilities. In 1990 there were 3.3 million Americans over the age of 84. By 2010 this number will grow to between 6.8 million and 8.3 million. These people obviously are the majority of the users of expensive lifesaving techniques, as well as nursing home facilities.

Between 1991 and 1992 alone, the cost of nursing home care rose by 12.5 percent—to $67.3 million—more than a full percentage point above health care costs in general.[6]

Are we as a nation willing to make the harsh decisions necessary to bring these costs down? If so, it will mean rationing health care services to our elderly.

In England, where the health care system has been touted as a sterling example of lower costs, those over 55 who need expensive medical care, such as dialysis, are routinely denied access. Age 55 doesn't seem old anymore.

Are we willing to have the government make this decision for us and our loved ones? Are we as a people going to practice eugenics, in which doctors who are responsible to government auditors make the decisions about who is allowed to live, based on their potential benefit to society?

From a statement made by Surgeon General Joycelyn Elders you can get a good feel for the attitude that is likely to prevail. "Abortion has an important and positive public effect," she commented during a lecture while she was the health chief in Arkansas.

By way of example, she pointed out that the number of Down's syndrome children in Washington state was 64 percent lower in 1976 than it would have been if abortion had not been legalized. In other words, the cost of a Down's syndrome child more than justifies his or her abortion.[7]

Transfer this same reasoning to national health care, and the effect on less-than-perfect human beings is virtually certain. It is estimated that the treatment cost of just one infant born addicted to drugs is $63,000. That's a "no-brainer" if we weigh only the costs.[8]

The cost of saving the life of a premature baby weighing less than three pounds at birth is estimated to be $165,000. That's an awful lot of office visits for the average taxpaying voter. Are we willing to say to the attending pediatrician, "You can spend up to $5,000 but no more"?

Will we be forced to adopt China's policy of aborting all potentially deformed or diseased babies? Think it can't happen here? Think again. Our government sends taxpayers' money around the world now to promote "family planning."[9]

Those who sneak past the abortion industry will face a government committee made up of bureaucrats and doctors who are committed to balancing the national health care budget in an election year.

I think of my own son, who was critically injured in a car accident in 1984. He had no medical insurance and accumulated more than $200,000 in medical expenses while in a coma. Virtually no attending physician gave him more than a 5 percent chance to live, and none gave him any realistic prospect of recovery. But because at the time of his accident the system still leaned more toward saving lives than meeting budgets, they continued to give him the best care possible.

Well, my son not only lived, he finished college, all his bills are paid in full, and he is a productive member of society. I doubt that he would have passed the scrutiny of a national health care review board.

If allowed to operate properly, the free market system eventually will bring costs into line through competition.

If the government really wants riots in the streets, one of the best ways to promote them is to deny lifesaving health care to those we love the most. Imagine the prospect of having your child denied a heart operation because some bureaucrat decides that, based on the child's social value to society, the cost is too high.

It is also important to bear in mind that health care costs are *not* what is sinking our economy. It is government irresponsibility. Does anyone honestly think that the same government that brought us $4.5 trillion in debt can reduce the costs of health care? If so, let the socialized medicine advocates practice on the Congress and federal employees first. If they survive, then maybe the rest of us should take a look at it.

In truth, as greater efforts have been made to control fees and technology use, the health care inflation rate has been coming down over the last several years. The rate of increase in medical prices has dropped by more than 30 percent in the last two years.[10]

If allowed to operate properly, the free market system eventually will bring costs into line through competition.

Actually what the government needs to do is *deregulate*, rather than increase regulation. If the government realistically wants to help to control costs, it needs to concentrate on making medical training accessible and affordable. Supply and demand soon will bring health care prices into reason, just as they have in the cost of televisions, food, clothing, and computers.

Irrespective of any other changes made, there is one vital key to reducing health care costs: consumer awareness. As long as patients don't see the cost of medicine coming out of their own pockets, there is little incentive to control these costs. Even now the vast majority of patients are covered by a fairly comprehensive health insurance plan. At most, they pay 10 to 20 percent of their health care bills.

Previously, employers provided health insurance with little or no deductibles at no cost to their employees. It has been only in the last few years that employers have been increasing the deductibles, co-payments, and passing along a share of the policy cost. Until this happened, the normal market-regulating forces were blunted.

It has been estimated that those who are covered by a comprehensive insurance plan "use 60 percent more physicians services and three times as much hospital care as those without policies."[11]

If we had a college tuition insurance plan fully paid by employers, there is no question that the cost of college would escalate beyond all reason, and no parent would bother to save toward that eventual need. The same basic attitude is at work in health care.

The alternative plans being presented in Congress generally focus on establishing individual medical IRAs, into which tax-exempt funds can be deposited and then used to pay medical expenses. One of the most succinct descriptions I have read was presented by Matthew Glavin, president of the Georgia Public Policy Foundation. Mr. Glavin's remarks were delivered before a Shavano Institute for National Leadership audience in Atlanta in May of 1993.

Individual Medical Accounts (IMAs) are [a] key to controlling health care costs and strengthening the role of the individual as a health care consumer. An Individual Medical Account would work like this: Individuals would be exempt from taxes on money deposited in an IMA, in the same way they currently pay no taxes on deposits to Individual Retirement Accounts (IRAs). Money to pay medical expenses could be withdrawn without penalty. . . .

Only about 10 percent of families in this country spend more than $2,000 per year on health care. This means 90 percent of all doctor visits would require no paperwork for insurance because they would be paid directly by the consumer out of the IMA. This also would increase consumer responsibility because there would be an incentive to control costs; the consumer keeps what he doesn't spend. . . .

Individual Medical Accounts would also be completely portable. One of the most serious problems of our current medical system is that insurance is so closely linked with employment. Individuals who lose their jobs or change jobs often lose their health insurance as well. Of the estimated 37 million Americans uninsured at any given time, half are without insurance for four months or less, and only 15 percent are uninsured for more than two years, but it still leaves them vulnerable, if only for a short time. With an IMA, individuals would continue to have funds available to pay for health care during temporary interruptions in employment.[12]

That concept is more compatible with our free enterprise system and virtually keeps the government out of medical care management.

One last comment on the cost of socializing the American medical system: The concept of mandatory employer/employee "contributions" to national health care does not reduce the cost of medicine. It simply makes it possible for the government to increase the contributions without having to go back to Congress for approval. If employers pay a percentage of all payroll into an alliance pool for health care, it is a tax—no matter how it's labeled.

In addition, the Clinton plan provides for the federal government to dictate to the states their "fair share" and levy a direct tax on businesses to cover it.

When employer and employee costs are combined, any reasonable national health care plan for a two-earner family with children will cost $5,800 a year or more. Also, every additional dollar in wages paid to a worker would carry a 7.9 percent employer tax and a 2.25 percent employee tax.[13]

In essence, we will simply create another runaway entitlement program that will punish employers, workers, and, most of all, future generations.

Martin Feldstein, President Reagan's chief economist, says the first-year cost of a national health care plan could run $120 billion *more* than the Clinton administration estimates.[14]

Thousands of companies will fail because they cannot absorb the increased costs or pass them along to their customers. When asked about this prospect, Hillary Clinton reportedly responded, "I can't go out and save every undercapitalized entrepreneur in America."[15]

> *As much as 25 percent of all health costs are related to liability related costs— including actual court costs, settlement costs, and defensive testing.*

That's easy for her to say. She'll be back in Arkansas, writing a book about how she singlehandedly saved the American health care system (which, by the way, retired presidents and their wives will not be required to join).

In the Fall of 1993, the first lady was asked by a woman insurance agent how the health care plan would affect the agent's job. Mrs. Clinton replied, "I'm assuming that anyone as obviously brilliant as you could find something else to market."[16]

Tell that to the 150,000 Americans who make their living selling health insurance. But at least they will have guaranteed coverage in their unemployment.

The issue that practically no one in the government is addressing is the cost of litigation to the health industry. Until, and unless, litigation is brought under control, costs *will not* be brought under control. It is estimated that as much as 25 percent of all health costs are related to liability related costs—including actual court costs, settlement costs, and defensive testing.[17]

Perhaps the reason the litigation issue is being avoided is that the majority of politicians are attorneys. They could be looking ahead to a time when they will lose their jobs and will need to rely on the litigation industry for their support. It seems to me I remember a parable the Lord gave us about an unrighteous steward who did something like that too.

THE UNINSURABLE

Guaranteed coverage is critical for those who are uninsurable through no fault of their own. I meet many such people as I travel and teach, and their stories are touching. People should not have their lives ruined and their financial futures jeopardized because they have developed a heart condition, cancer, or some other disease that renders them a bad risk.

It's also hard to fault the insurance companies who decline to insure high-risk people. After all, the insurance companies have to make a profit to stay in business. It would be an irresponsible company that would write a health insurance policy on an AIDS patient who was facing $200,000 to $300,000 in medical expenses over a 5-year period when, at the same time, that patient would be paying only about $6,000 a year in premiums.

All of these people can be covered (as they are now) by spreading the cost over the vast majority of healthy people. No one I have talked to says that seriously ill people who don't have insurance are denied medical attention anywhere in the country. If they are treated in private hospitals, their costs are averaged into the bills of paying patients. Any hospital that accepts any form of government aid—grants, loans, Medicaid, Medicare—cannot legally refuse to treat indigent patients.

WHAT ABOUT THE 38.5 MILLION UNINSURED?

Are there really 38.5 million uninsured Americans? Many people believe the actual number is but a fraction of the notorious 38.5 million usually touted by the administration as justification for socialized health care. (In his 1994 State of the Union message, the president claimed the number is 58 million.)

When the figures are broken down, we find that about one-half of the uninsured are actually in transition from one job to another. They generally will be unemployed for one year or less. These people would be covered, as previously discussed, by having their insurance and medical IRAs portable.

Another six million or so of the uninsured are people who were offered health insurance and declined to take it because they had to pay something out of their own pocket. Typically, these are young workers who don't think they're going to get sick and would rather spend their money elsewhere. They would profit from the medical IRA if they were allowed to keep (tax free) the residual in their accounts each year. A condition to receiving this benefit would be that they had to purchase a major medical policy to cover catastrophic health care costs. This would take care of another six million or so uninsured.[18]

Ultimately, the system is left with perhaps six- to seven-million truly uninsured or uninsurable people. Two questions must be answered: Why are they uninsurable? and, Do we really want to cover everyone in our society? What about those who could care less about their own health and actively engage in high-risk activities like prostitution, homosexuality, drugs, alcohol, and gang activities?

Would the average American consider paying more for his or her own car liability insurance so that drunk drivers would not have to pay more for their car insurance?

Is it fair that a computer company should have to pay more for their workers' compensation insurance so that a mining company wouldn't have to pay more? And should a family living in an Anaheim, California subdivision pay more for their homeowners' policy so that those living in high fire- and flood-risk areas won't have to pay more?

Should the pilot of a private airplane be charged more than someone who never flies a small plane? Isn't that discrimination based on risk? Sure it is, and rightly so.

We already have seen the effect of removing all responsibility from certain classes in our society. The result is a teen pregnancy epidemic, crime in the cities, criminals' rights promoted above their victims' rights, and a lower standard of living for our society as a whole.

At some point, common sense has to be restored to our society. We easily can provide health insurance for those who are uninsured because of a job loss, bad health, accidents, or birth defects. What we cannot and should not do is send a message that the more irresponsible a person is the more benefits he or she is entitled to.

The apostle Paul had some profound wisdom for our generation in 2 Thessalonians 3:10. *"For even when we were with you, we used to give you this order: if anyone will not work, neither let him eat."*

ABORTION INSURANCE

Without a doubt, one of the major objectives of the Clinton administration is to provide abortion payments as a part of the Health Security Act. When questioned about this provision, Hillary Clinton responded, "We're striking the right balance [on this issue]." Doctors and hospitals morally opposed to abortion could decide to opt out, she claimed.[19]

In the first place, I rather suspect that, if abortion is accepted as a "necessary benefit," there would be heavy pressure put on those who oppose abortion to participate or be subjected to financial penalties. It's kind of like telling the public, "Sure you can select your own doctor," and then making it a criminal offense for doctors to treat patients outside of their assigned group.

Christians will have to take a stand on this issue, regardless of the consequences. We should have acted with one voice when the Supreme Court decided that somehow an unborn human has no rights. Once abortion is funded through a national health care plan, the number of abortions likely will escalate.

God's people must wake up to this offense now! There is no nation that will survive God's wrath for long, if and when it decides to kill its young (and old).

NOTES

1. Robert Rector, "Exposing the Federal Welfare Racket," *Dimensions*, 2/93.
2. White House Domestic Policy Council, *The President's Health Security Plan*, New York: Times Books, 1993, pp. 10, 199-201; Grace-Marie Arnett, "Cops and Doctors," *The Washington Post*, 12/19/93.
3. Robert E. Bauman, "The V.A.'s War on Health," *The Wall Street Journal*, 12/6/93.
4. Gary Robbins, Aldona Robbins, and John Goodman, "How Our Health Care System Works," National Center for Policy Analysis, Report No. 177, 2/93; Robert W. Lee, "Creating the Crisis," *The New American*, 11/1/93, pp. 19-25.
5. Dana Priest, "Health Plan's Five-Year Cost Estimated at $700 Billion," *Washington Post*, 9/10/93.
6. J. D. Kleinke, "The Health Care Inflation Fantasy," *The Wall Street Journal*, 10/18/93.

7. Nat Hentoff, "A Surgeon General Who Accepts Eugenics?", *Washington Post,* 8/21/93.

8. Elizabeth McCaughey, "Health Plan's Devilish Details," *The Wall Street Journal,* 9/30/93.

9. John M. Goshko, "A.I.D. Awards Planned Parenthood Grant," *Washington Post,* 11/23/93; Thomas W. Lippman, "Population Control Is Called a 'Top Priority' in Foreign Policy," *Washington Post,* 1/12/94.

10. Paul Sperry, "The Health Care 'Crisis' Myth," *Investor's Business Daily,* 10/25/93.

11. Doug Bandow, "The High Cost of Nationalized Medical Care," *Conservative Chronicle,* 9/27/93, p. 7.

12. Matthew J. Glavin, "Health Care and a Free Society," *Imprimis,* the monthly journal of Hillsdale College, 11/93.

13. Martin Feldstein, "Clinton's Hidden Health Tax," *The Wall Street Journal,* 11/10/93.

14. Clay Chandler and Spencer Rich, "Clinton Challenged on Health Plan's Cost, Impact," *Washington Post,* 9/24/93.

15. *McAlvany Intelligence Advisor,* 11/93, p. 22.

16. Greg Steinmetz, "Clinton Health Plan Casualty: The Health Insurance Agent," *The Wall Street Journal,* 11/17/93.

17. Jesse Malkin, "Health Care's Ignored Problem," *Investor's Business Daily,* 10/27/93.

18. Greg Steinmetz, "Number of Uninsured Stirs Much Confusion in Health Care Debate," *The Wall Street Journal,* 6/09/93.

19. Karen Ball, "Health-Abortion," *The Associated Press,* 9/24/93.

17
NAFTA

Since the North American Free Trade Agreement (NAFTA) was passed in 1993, it is worthy of discussing its economic impact on the country. Most assuredly there will be an effect, both short term and long term.

NAFTA was one of those perplexing issues for many Americans who couldn't decide whether they were for it or against it. Who wouldn't have been confused? We saw conservative Republicans lining up behind a liberal Democratic president who was willing to alienate his major support group (unions) to get this bill through the Congress.

Any thinking person should have wondered why Bill Clinton would risk incurring the wrath of the unions and his own party to pass a treaty that was negotiated, in large part, by the Republican president he had just defeated. I don't think the reason is all that complicated—once you understand what NAFTA really does.

NAFTA really has three distinct goals, each of which appeals to one group or the other.

THE ECONOMIC SIDE OF NAFTA

It was the basic economic ideals of NAFTA that attracted the conservatives who generally stand for free trade, meaning a lowering of tariffs between nations. It was this element of NAFTA that was negotiated by George Bush and his staff.

Free trade with an underdeveloped country like Mexico means huge savings for businesses that can take advantage of the cheaper labor force without paying the penalty of higher tariffs meant to equalize the cost differences. Free trade with an underdeveloped country usually means a net loss of jobs in the more developed economies—like the U.S. and Canada.

In reality, NAFTA is not a free trade agreement because many tariffs are maintained for as long as 20 years. This is particularly true of tariffs placed on some American products that could be sold in Mexico. But since our government rarely negotiates anything for Americans on an equal basis, this is not unusual.

It was the economic (tariff reduction) side of NAFTA that attracted most of the conservatives. But even many of them objected to an agreement to lower trade barriers that required some 1,300 pages of complicated language. It seemed to me, and others I discussed this with, that the entire agreement could have been summarized in three or four pages—max!

If God gave us the Ten Commandments in two pages you'd think we could lower tariffs between Canada, Mexico, and the U.S. in four pages. But complexity usually comes from hiring too many lawyers to work in Washington.

It is quite possible that some of the complicated language associated with NAFTA will come back to haunt Americans as the agreements are reinterpreted over the years. But, in reality, that is true of any agreement or law drafted in Washington today. Just look at how the Supreme Court has adulterated the simple language of the Constitution.

It was my observation, when NAFTA was being debated, that a conservative could argue for or against the agreement, based solely on its economic merits.

In the short run, there almost certainly will be a loss of jobs in the U.S. as companies migrate to Mexico to take advantage of their cheaper labor, lower taxes, and virtually no regulations. In my opinion, anyone who tries to argue that NAFTA will not encourage American companies to move to Mexico has never lived in the real world.

American companies already were migrating south before NAFTA was signed, even though many of their products were subject to high tariffs upon reentering the United States. The reason these companies moved to Mexico was fairly simple: The cost of labor and benefits in the U.S. exceeded the cost of tariffs.

In addition, many companies simply could not continue to operate under current U.S. environmental and labor laws profitably. Mexico and other underdeveloped nations offered these companies reasonably low-cost alternatives. Some companies relocated to Korea, Taiwan, or China. Others chose to invest in Mexico simply because of its proximity to the U.S. and the fact that NAFTA was at least a possibility.

With the tariff problem all but eliminated, as a result of NAFTA, it is reasonable to expect that many more companies will migrate south—some into the U.S. from Canada because labor costs and taxes in Canada are higher than ours; and many more will migrate from the U.S. to Mexico. As more capital is poured into Mexico and the infrastructure is improved, we likely will see other countries locate plants there—to escape the duties and tariffs placed on their products entering the U.S.

It appears that our government is purposely trying to force American industry to relocate somewhere else.

In the short run, NAFTA is almost certain to cost Americans jobs, especially in the low and semi-skilled ranks. Perhaps a decade or two from now Mexico will be a viable trading partner and wages and benefits will have equalized, as ours come down and theirs go up, but several hundred thousand American workers will not find jobs—unless they sneak across the border into Mexico.

If this were 1974, we could absorb the loss of jobs, just as we did when most of our electronics industry shifted to Japan. But with fewer jobs being created already, the loss of jobs will be sorely felt, especially among manufacturing and assembly workers.

Certainly we will sell many of our products in Mexico. But the Mexican middle class is not the same as the U.S. middle class. Their average hourly wage is slightly over $2, and ours is nearly $10. This means our product sales will be high volume discount goods, produced by highly automated techniques. The profits may be good but, in reality, few jobs will be created to produce them.

On the other hand, textiles, automobiles, paper products, and other labor-intensive goods will face virtually impossible competition from Mexico's cheap labor force. Interestingly enough, in the Northern U.S. the Canadian labor force faces a somewhat equivalent threat from the U.S. side. We're high priced and over-regulated, but nothing like Canada.

Anytime our Supreme Court can reinterpret the Constitution to provide legal protection for abortion and pornography, any interpretation is quite possible.

In reality, if our government would stop over-regulating businesses and burdening companies with more and more mandated benefits, there would be less incentive for a mass exodus of U.S. companies to relocate across the Mexican border. But it appears that our government is purposely trying to force American industry to relocate somewhere else. The one positive side of NAFTA is that it's better for U.S. companies to move to Mexico than China, which many are doing now.

THE SOVEREIGNTY SIDE OF NAFTA

One aspect of NAFTA is to establish a series of tri-lateral commissions, made up of U.S., Mexican, and Canadian regulators, to ensure that all of the agreements are adhered to by each nation.

A common complaint voiced by strict constitutionalists during the NAFTA debates was that NAFTA rules enforced by these commissions could supersede the U.S. Constitution. By strict rule of international law, virtually any treaty can supersede any signatory nation's Constitution if the two conflict. But if national sovereignty is threatened, the NAFTA agreement makes provision for any nation to withdraw.

Will NAFTA be used to negate some of the constitutional rights of Americans? Nobody really knows at this time. Given the past track record of our lawmakers to reinterpret anything written, I would not doubt it. But, in reality, that also holds true for the several dozen other treaties to which we are a party.

The environmental protection is a tool being used to spread the big government agenda of the activists in the Clinton administration.

Anytime our Supreme Court can reinterpret the Constitution to provide legal protection for abortion and pornography, any interpretation is quite possible.

During the debate on NAFTA, Judge Robert Bork gave his evaluation of NAFTA in regard to national sovereignty and concluded that it represented no greater threat than any other such treaty in the past. I defer to his wisdom and knowledge on this issue.

THE ENVIRONMENTAL SIDE OF NAFTA

Although President Bush negotiated the major portion of the NAFTA agreement, President Clinton negotiated what are called the supplemental, or side, agreements. These side agreements are also an integral part of NAFTA and were approved at the time NAFTA itself was approved. In my opinion, it is the side agreements that pose the greatest danger to our economy, and they are the reason President Clinton pushed so hard to get NAFTA approved.

Like any government document, these side agreements are not simple to understand. Supposedly, the side agreements were negotiated to overcome some of the concerns expressed by NAFTA opponents. But since most of the NAFTA opponents were members of the president's own party who still didn't vote for the treaty, that argument does not hold much water.

The side agreements alone contain more than 43 pages of clarifications, many of which are ambiguous and rambling. But one particular aspect stood out as I read the supplemental agreements—Article 5: Government Enforcement Action.

It was thought by many constitutionalists that the danger of NAFTA side agreements was that they would allow Mexico or Canada to dictate terms to American companies in deference to state or federal constitutions. That is not the real danger.

It is important to understand that the environmental protection (meaning more regulations) is a tool being used to spread the big government agenda of the activists in the Clinton administration. NAFTA will help them to lock in these environmental regulations forever!

Under Ronald Reagan much of the government's regulatory ability was dismantled—to the ire of the environmentalists. The Bush administration reestablished a great deal of the regulatory capabilities of the federal government, but was constrained somewhat by the Council on Competitiveness, headed by Vice President Quayle, which looked at the possible economic impact of proposed regulations.

One of the Clinton administration's first actions was to do away with the Council. Fortunately, some members of Congress are trying to pass a law that would require such economic impact studies.

Some analysts believe that under a strict interpretation of the NAFTA supplemental agreement on the environment, no signing nation can reduce its current level of environmental protection. That does not particularly affect Mexico, because it has very few regulations. But for the United States, it means that our current environmental regulations (plus any that are added) are locked in, and no subsequent administration or Congress can lower them without violating the terms of NAFTA.

These side agreements can do more to destroy the economy of the U.S. than all the rest of NAFTA combined. Articles 22, 23, 24 and 31-36 of the supplemental agreements define the means of enforcing these provisions. It was no accident that strict environmental regulation enforcement became an integral part of NAFTA. The American people have been duped again.

Combined with the Clinton tax policy, the pending Health Security Act, and the current state of our national debt, it is very difficult to be extremely optimistic about the future of our economy. It's hard to see how anyone could do so many things to undermine our economy simply by accident.

18

QUESTIONS AND ANSWERS

U sually when I discuss the topic of the coming economic earthquake at a conference or on our radio program someone will ask when I'm going to publish a list of the most commonly asked questions and answers. Well, here they are.

I don't pretend to have all the answers or, perhaps, even all the questions. I have purposely omitted the questions that asked specifically where to invest funds. To cover any investment strategy in a book like *The Coming Economic Earthquake* would be an exercise in futility—both for you and for me. I often discuss investment strategy but not specific companies or products. A previous book titled *Investing for the Future* (Victor Books) covers the majority of these specific questions. There are many other excellent books about investing in your local Christian bookstore.

Perhaps the best way to diversify for most average income investors is through mutual funds. A good friend, Austin Pryor, has written a book titled *Sound Mind Investing* (Moody Press), which I believe is one of the best ever written on this topic.

QUESTIONS AND ANSWERS

1. What is the difference between the deficit and the national debt?

The annual deficit is the amount our government spends each year in excess of what it generates through all sources of income—taxes, tariffs, fees. The national debt is merely the accumulation of all the annual deficits.

2. How is the national debt funded?

The national debt and the annual deficits are funded by government borrowing: our government borrows issuing Treasury bills, Treasury bonds, and other letters of credit for which it pays interest.

3. To whom do we owe this debt?

The vast majority of the debt is owed to Americans who have purchased government securities—either personally or through a local bank, mutual fund, pension account, or other financial institution. About 18 to 20 percent of the public debt is actually held by foreign interests, the largest portion being held by Europeans.

4. Why worry about the debt? We seem to be handling it okay now, and many economists say too much attention is being given to paying back our debt. Some say paying off the debt actually would hurt our economy.

I have heard most of the positive comments about the national debt and, in reality, it is not the actual debt that is our major problem. It is the continued accumulation of yearly deficits that just keep growing. Every dollar the government takes to fund its overspending is a dollar that will never be available to start a business or create a real job.

As of 1990 the government was borrowing approximately 58 percent of the annual savings of all Americans. In four or five years it could borrow 100 percent, leaving nothing for new businesses except the capital that is already in circulation.

I would submit that the debt does matter—especially when the annual deficit exceeds the ability of our government to fund it, as it will eventually if not brought under control. If the national debt really doesn't matter, why not eliminate all taxes and just borrow what the government needs each year? Most taxpayers would support that idea.

The same rules that apply to families and businesses apply to our government also: You can't spend more than you make forever.

5. What actually will happen when the government can't pay its bills?

No one knows for sure, but based on the history of other economies where this has happened, services were drastically reduced, federal employees were laid off, taxes were increased dramatically and, eventually, those governments resorted to printing money to pay their bills. Once that happened, inflation roared to life.

If too much money is printed too quickly, and that depends on the amount of unfunded deficit, hyperinflation can occur.

Hyperinflation occurs when confidence in a nation's currency is undermined worldwide and rapid devaluation takes place. Again, how much the money is devalued depends, in large part, on the confidence bond traders have in that country's leadership and their ability to control future monetizing (printing new money).

In the case of our country, the confidence of most Americans in their government leaders to solve problems is very low today. If the average American loses confidence in the dollar and begins to dump fixed investments, such as T-bills, the value of our currency could plummet quickly.

6. Why can't we eliminate the deficit by increasing revenue and cutting government spending?

We absolutely can—theoretically. But discipline is not one of the long suits in Washington these days. When taxes were lowered in the eighties and government revenues increased, instead of using the revenue to reduce the deficit, spending was increased.

By the way, the government actually received more money in taxes as a result of President Reagan's tax cuts in 1981. Unfortunately, for every additional dollar received, it spent an additional $1.68; thus, the deficits actually got worse with more money. In counseling we call this "the more money in equals the more money out" syndrome.

Virtually all of the spending cuts we have heard about in the last 10 years actually have been decreases in the amount of additional spending the government was *planning* to do. No serious plan submitted thus far by the majority party has suggested cutting current levels of spending—or even holding future spending to current levels.

Without this level of commitment, there is no solution. More revenue will not help the deficits until actual spending cuts are made.

7. If the deficits are really bad, why are interest rates staying so low?

It's interesting to me to hear our president take credit for the low interest rates, as if they represent an administrative achievement. I like the low interest rates too because they allow many families the opportunity to buy homes and eliminate old, high interest loans. But, in reality, low interest rates reflect an anemic economy with little or no growth in the small business sector.

Interest rates are highly subject to supply-and-demand forces: The greater the demand, the higher the rates, and vice versa. Obviously the Federal Reserve Board also can artificially manipulate interest rates to combat some of the inflation created by government expansion of the money supply. But the low interest rates are due, in large part, to an anemic worldwide economy.

Interest rates generally will stay down until economic activity picks up. Our government is doing very little to stimulate economic growth and a great deal to retard it. The current interest rates merely reflect that.

8. Why is inflation so low if we are facing an economic earthquake?

Basically, for the same reasons I have just outlined: The economy is weak, and retailers have a very difficult time passing along their increased costs to consumers. In many cases they would not sell anything if current prices really reflected current costs.

Just look at the airline industry. The majority of companies are actually operating at a loss, but they find themselves unable to increase fares because of stiff competition from start-up companies with low overhead.

Oil producers are actually selling crude oil at less than production costs just to generate cash flow. This major component of our economy (oil prices) is working for Bill Clinton, just as it worked against Jimmy Carter in the seventies.

In the short run most consumers benefit from deflation, since their dollars go further. But deflation also means fewer jobs and less economic growth. If allowed to run its full course, deflation easily can turn into depression. If it were not for artificial government spending (deficit spending), we would be in a major down cycle. The question is: How long can we deficit spend, raise taxes, and still maintain a viable economy? Not forever. That's for sure.

9. *You encourage people to pay off debt, even their homes if possible. But what good will that do if we have an economic earthquake? And if we have hyperinflation, wouldn't it be better to owe a lot of money? We could pay it back with cheaper dollars.*

Allow me to address the second question first. If during an inflationary cycle your income could stay even or ahead of inflation, then it might make sense to load up on debt in prospect of paying it back with cheaper dollars. But it almost never happens that way. Usually income lags inflation substantially, and mandatory expenses consume ever-greater percentages of your disposable income.

In Argentina and Brazil, inflation eventually consumed virtually all of most average families' income just in increased food and utility costs. We're seeing the same situation in Russia today. Most fixed income people, such as retirees, were wiped out financially in just a few months. And average income families spend all they make on food and utilities.

Now to your first question—about getting out of debt. If you get out of debt, you can begin building up a surplus.

Those who have a surplus of funds should already be helping others in need and should be planning how to help even more during some really dark days. To do this requires that assets be invested wisely, including investing outside of the U.S.

The greater the amount of assets available, the greater diversification that can be achieved. But no diversification is possible if you adopt a spend-it-now philosophy.

10. If we are truly facing an economic earthquake, is it better not to buy a home if we can't pay cash for it?

In my opinion, if you can buy a home, with a mortgage payment reasonably close to what you are currently paying in rent, it is still better to buy. Rent is as much a monthly obligation as a mortgage, and you can never pay off rent. At least with a mortgage you have a chance to accumulate some equity and control your monthly expenses.

My counsel has never been either/or advice—meaning either pay off your mortgage or don't buy a home. But I believe that it is better to own a home with no mortgage, if you can.

11. For years my husband has been worrying about the future of our economy. It has driven him to hoarding, and he has become stingy about everything. He is not willing to allow me to buy even a new chair. We have hundreds of thousands of dollars in investments, but he still insists on more savings. I think he is overreacting, and now it's impossible to enjoy life around him. Can you give me some advice?

It is truly sad that some people live in fear of the future. That is not at all what I teach or counsel. Anything taken to an extreme can be harmful to our relationship with God and our families.

I truly believe Christians should become debt free, save something for the future, and help others, but it should be done in balance. It sounds like your husband has been trapped by his fear into trying to protect himself against any eventuality. That simply is not possible.

It is also very possible that what you are seeing is an outside indicator that he does not know the Lord in a personal way and is relying on material things for his security.

As Proverbs 18:11 says, *"A rich man's wealth is his strong city, and like a high wall in his own imagination."*

If I were counseling your husband I probably would give him advice that runs contrary to much of what I would give others. He should give the vast majority of what he has away (with your input also). To him, his riches have become a snare from Satan. He needs to learn to trust God, instead of his stored wealth.

12. *In the event of a coming economic earthquake, would I be better off with assets like gold and real estate instead of paper investments like mutual funds and bonds?*

That is very difficult to say. In the past, fixed assets such as gold and silver have always held their value relative to other assets. Whether or not that will be the case in the next crisis is hard to say. In my opinion, they will do well, particularly in a hyperinflationary period, simply because precious metals are still recognized as standards of value by most investors worldwide.

Typically, gold represents the more stable asset in times of economic difficulty. If I had more than $100,000 in assets, I certainly would have some of it in gold and silver. What portion is the right balance? I don't know, but most investment advisors I spoke to who don't sell precious metals themselves thought about 5 to 10 percent would be the correct balance.

Investments in real estate tend to do well in inflationary periods and not do so well during deflationary periods. The trick is to determine when one period is changing to the other. Unless you understand real estate investments well, you probably should use professional advice. Perhaps investing through mutual funds that specialize in residential development companies would be your best direction.

13. *Your suggestion that government might confiscate private retirement accounts for their use frightens me. Should I begin pulling some money out of these accounts, even though I will have to pay a penalty?*

243

I still firmly believe that in years to come the government will, in its relentless search for funds, convert many retirement accounts to public use.

We already see some of this happening as public pension funds are being tapped for investments in the inner cities. Presently there is some $4 trillion stored in tax-deferred accounts by American workers. It has been my observation that when the politicians give you something (tax deferment) they somehow tend to think of that money as being theirs.

I would not encourage anyone to cash out their retirement accounts—certainly not at this point anyway. We will have plenty of warning if and when the government decides to convert or confiscate retirement savings, as is now being done with Social Security trust funds.

However, I believe anyone would be well advised to pay the current taxes on at least one-half of all designated retirement funds and invest them outside of retirement accounts. There are some very good tax deferred annuities that will allow the funds to grow, undiminished by taxes but still held outside of traditional retirement accounts, such as 401(K)s, IRAs, and pension plans.

14. In what ways have you correctly (or incorrectly) predicted the direction in our economy?

That's a fair question. First I must say that I have always hedged by saying that I am not a prophet. All I ever try to do is look at the past, look at the present, and try to guess the future direction of our economy.

The longer I live, the more I realize that correctly projecting timing in our economy is virtually impossible. If we were following the basic rules of supply and demand taught by Adam Smith, then we could get a clearer picture of the future; but we are not.

The Federal Reserve can manipulate the money supply to counteract many market conditions, thus creating artificial inflation or deflation in the money supply. This totally confuses the future picture because you not only have to read the market but also the minds of the Reserve Board members—not to mention the president, the Congress, and the voters.

I thought in the early seventies that we would see hyperinflation by the late seventies or early eighties. In fact, we did see a high rate of inflation, caused in large part by skyrocketing oil prices, not expansion of the money supply.

I also thought the economy would suffer a significant downturn in the late seventies as the Fed attempted to control inflation through high interest rates. This did happen, and the recession it created forced President Jimmy Carter out of office and ushered in Ronald Reagan. Who would have expected a very conservative Republican president to be elected so soon after the Nixon fiasco? I know I didn't.

Ronald Reagan ushered in the most productive business cycle in this century—including the Roaring Twenties. Even though we had a lot of debt expansion throughout the economy, we had even more real economic growth. We simply outran inflation and allowed the economy to grow faster than the increasing money supply.

Unfortunately, we are now in a condition in which the debt is expanding faster than the economy. This means fewer jobs, higher unemployment and, more recently, higher income taxes.

Our economy is struggling between two forces: free enterprise, which requires a great deal of free choice and risk to thrive, and fascism, which allows private ownership but almost total government control. In my opinion, if this fascism is allowed to expand, our economy simply will fold under this load of debt and regulation, and either we will have a massive depression or, more probably, hyperinflation as the government prints money to pay its bills.

How accurate have my projections been? Probably about as accurate as they have been in the past. I cannot project timing very well but, in the long run, true economic principles take over. Not even the Fed can overrule the laws of economics: Spend more than you make and you will eventually run out of money.

15. *If we truly do have an economic earthquake, won't we have riots in the streets and gangs pillaging our homes? Should we plan to leave the country during this period?*

The scenario you pose is frightening and one that I hesitate to comment on. It is quite possible that if our economy gets bad enough we will have riots. Thus far we have seen the riots limited to only inner-city ghettos. But if they expand beyond the angry inner-city poor to the working poor, we could see riots on a scale unimaginable by most law-abiding citizens.

The reality of this can be seen in the millions of guns sold to normal, non-violent citizens each year. The trend in gun sales is exponential now and rising constantly. This is a sign that those living within reach of violent criminals sense the rising anger as well.

The fact the criminals who burned and pillaged their own communities were treated like oppressed victims of their environment does nothing to reassure Americans that our government has their best interests at heart. The advocacy groups are there to be sure the rights of the criminals are not violated. Law abiding citizens feel that no one is protecting their rights. That's why they are stocking up on guns.

Having said all that, I still would say to God's people: The Lord knows our needs. He will provide what we need in the midst of chaos. I believe we will have an opportunity to witness to millions of otherwise apathetic Americans. God didn't raise up an army of followers only to have us abdicate before the battle.

I have to be honest and say that I am concerned for those who live in and near the big cities. Crime is out of control now. With any provocation, it can rage through the suburbs quickly. Unless criminals are made to believe that swift and sure punishment awaits them, they will get bolder. Our criminal justice system has been underminded by the liberal federal courts. It's time to insist that justice be put back into the courtroom. When God's laws and punishments are removed from a society, we see the result. The answer is to elect men and women who value these timeless principles. But, more than anything, we need revival in the hearts of Americans of all races, classes, and theologies.

16. *I don't see any long-term security in working for a large company any more. The company I work for had a 50-year history of no layoffs, but now new management is laying off tens of thousands of middle-aged workers and replacing*

them with young, lower-salaried workers. I don't want that to happen to me in 20 years. Is this a good time to think about starting my own business?

The trend in corporate America toward downsizing is a normal market adjustment to lower demand and increased competition from countries with cheaper labor. It is unfortunate that the business climate created by excessive regulation makes it more difficult to start the new businesses that should be creating the jobs these displaced workers need. The problem is not the downsizing. It is the lack of new businesses taking up the slack.

Downsizing is not unusual or abnormal in economic cycles. When steam trains came into wide production, stage coach manufacturers downsized. When automobiles went into mass production, carriage manufacturers downsized. When electric lights came into common use, gas lantern companies downsized.

The big difference between past downsizing and now is that our politicians are so fearful of the social and environmental activists they are willing to kill future industrial growth to prove they are "politically correct." Consequently, it is more difficult to start new industries in America.

I would encourage you to look carefully at the business you are considering. If it involves chemicals, you will be facing increasing regulation. The same can be said of any business even remotely related to minerals, lumbering, refrigeration, and . . . the list could go on and on.

If you are starting your own business, if at all possible, be certain you have enough capital to last at least one full year without drawing any income from the business. In the final analysis, going into business for yourself is still the best way to accumulate wealth in America. I would encourage anyone who has the talent and managerial abilities to start a business to do it.

At the same time, we need to rein in this regulatory madness that is destroying our economic foundation. The way you do that is by voting out the politicians who vote to destroy the futures of our children and grandchildren.

19

SUMMARY OF WHERE WE ARE

I t is hard to imagine any action that our government could take that would affect our economy more adversely than to attempt to nationalize our health care system. Not only has the federal government demonstrated time and again its ineptness in controlling costs and operating anything efficiently but, in fact, they have continued to set the standards for inefficiency, bureaucracy, complexity, and cost.

Look at any area the government has touched and see if you can say honestly it is cheaper, more efficient, and less complicated. If so, please write me so I can put the information in the next book.

While other countries are desperately trying to privatize government-run agencies to avert financial ruin, we are trying to socialize another one-seventh of our whole economy!

Based on what is happening in Washington today, I have concluded that no real changes are being made to bring federal spending under control. Consequently, it is my conclusion that sometime prior to the end of this century we will experience a severe financial downturn caused by taxes that are too high, too much debt, too much regulation, and too many Americans on government "dole."

Perhaps this downturn (recession) will be precipitated by a stock market crisis, as in 1929, or perhaps the stock market crisis will follow the downturn. The two are not necessarily directly related.

The recession will expand into a depression as businesses fail, unemployment rises, and consumer confidence plummets. Even so, taxes will be increased to feed an ever-expanding program of government supplied entitlements. The government will soon exhaust the last available resources as they tax all benefits, raid retirement savings, and eliminate the remaining middle income deductions. Politicians will be caught in a catch 22.

The more they tax, the lower the net gain in taxes and the more Americans are put out of work. With fewer available wage earners to tax, taxes are raised again. Finally, when taxes and credit are exhausted, the government will resort to the ultimate debt reduction plan: inflation—soon to be followed by hyperinflation, as the government attempts to print its way out of debt.

I don't want to sound like an alarmist, but I do want to sound an alarm: This health care plan can destroy the foundation of our free enterprise system all by itself.

As noted previously, this condition has been a prelude to several despots who plunged their nations into war. We again see that situation developing in Russia. Can it happen in America too? That basically depends on how bad the economy gets for the average American.

These problems would be desperate enough if we were living in the American society of 30 years ago, but in our society, where crime and riots are commonplace, the consequences could be a loss of personal freedoms in the name of restoring order.

In 1990, President Bush responded to our economic problems in the best manner of Herbert Hoover and succeeded in surrendering the White House to Bill Clinton. Since January 20th, 1993, the Clinton administration has been on a course to expand the New Deal into the "Bad Deal."

I believe our economy will begin to show the effects of the latest tax increase in late 1994 or early 1995. Hopefully we can absorb the net loss of capital in the private sector without slumping into a depression as we did the 1930s. We'll just have to wait and see how resilient our economy is.

It is interesting that most of the industrialized world is in the midst of a major recession, just as they were in 1932-33. The U.S. led the way then with bad economic policies, and the rest of the world followed us into the economic abyss of the thirties. We appear to be practicing what could be called one-upmanship and trying to outdo the New Deal.

The national Health Security Act is beyond anything ever imagined, even by Franklin Delano Roosevelt. The bureaucracy created to administer health care will equal the total federal bureaucracy that already exists in any department of the government.

I have reprinted a copy of Congressman Dick Armey's flow chart, which depicts the bureaucracy outlined by this plan. If you can follow the chart on the next page, you should probably apply for a job in Washington.

I don't want to sound like an alarmist, but I do want to sound an alarm: This health care plan can destroy the foundation of our free enterprise system all by itself. If we didn't have the problems of over-regulation of business, runaway entitlement programs, an aging population, 30 million abortions sapping our consumer and tax base, excessive litigation threatening every viable business, and a $12 trillion debt ($4.5 trillion on-budget, and $6 to $8 trillion off-budget), this health care plan still would threaten our economic future.

It's quite possible that a massive program like this, at such a crucial juncture in our economy, will be the trigger to collapse our economy. I don't know how to say this any stronger without

Clinton Health Care Plan

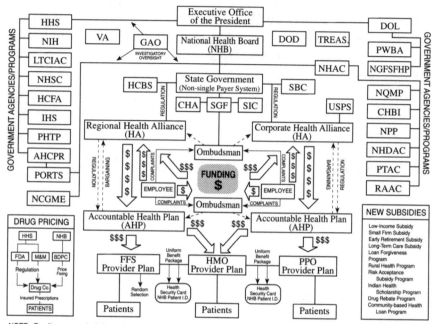

NOTE: Funding sources include employer 7.9% tax, employee AHC tax, nonworker and P/T worker tax, other taxes, and M&M savings.

AHCPR: Agency for Health Care Policy and Research
AHP: Accountable Health Plan
BDPC: Breakthrough Drug Pricing Committee
CHA: County Health Authorities
CHBI: Commission on Health Benefits and Integration
DOD: Department of Defense
DOL: Department of Labor
FDA: Food and Drug Administration
FFS: Fee for Service Provider Plan
GAO: General Accounting Office
HA: Health Alliances
HCBS: Home and Community-Based Services
HCFA: Health Care Financing Administration
HHS: Department of Health and Human Services
HMO: Health Maintenance Organization
IHS: Indian Health Services
LTCIAC: Long-Term Care Insurance Advisory Council
M&M: Medicare and Medicaid
NCGME: National Council on Graduate Medical Education
NGFSFHP: National Guaranty Fund for Self-Funded Health Plans

NHAC: National Health Advisory Committees
NHB: National Health Board
NHDAC: National Health Data Advisory Council
NHSC: National Health Service Corps
NIH: National Institutes of Health
NPP: National Privacy Panel
NQMP: National Quality Management Program
PHTP: Priority Health Training Programs
PORTs: Patient Outcome Research Teams
PPO: Preferred Provider Organizations
PTAC: Premium Target Advisory Commission
PWBA: Pension Welfare and Benefits Administration
RAAC: Risk Adjustment Advisory Committee
SBC: School Based Clinics
SGF: State Guaranty Funds
SIC: State Insurance Commission
TREAS: Treasury Department
USPS: U.S. Postal Service
VA: Department of Veterans Affairs

Source: Rep. Dick Armey, House Republican Conference

sounding offensive: It is, beyond any doubt, government bureaucracy at its worst.

I am sure, as many of my friends in Congress are, that some form of national health care will be passed—modified for sure—but still left intact enough to ruin our small business base.

I would like to summarize some of the most critical aspects of the proposed health care plan. Hopefully, many of you will have a chance to let your representatives in Washington know how you feel before this thing becomes law.

1. Total funding will require additional spending of perhaps $150 billion a year when totally implemented—by the end of this decade. Some of this will be paid by direct taxes, such as the cigarette tax, but the majority will be paid by employers and employees, in an approximate 80/20 ratio as an off-budget entitlement. This translates into a payroll tax of about 8 percent for employers and a personal (non-deductible) tax of 2 to 4 percent for all employees.[1]

   Administration officials say that only about 30 percent of Americans will actually pay more than they do right now. Remember, when income taxes were authorized (in 1914), we were promised that the maximum tax would be one percent and only on incomes above $20,000.[2]

   All employers will be responsible for their portion of employees' health care. That means if you hire a child care worker, maid, or gardener, you pay a portion of that person's health care!

2. In order to meet any reasonable semblance of a budget, price controls will be instituted. The only effective price controls available to the government are those provided by rationing. This means long waits for treatment and services.

   In England, for instance, the average wait for surgery is seven months. Those who know how to use the system expect waits at doctors' offices of up to eight hours; so they arrive early, take their number, and go out to do their shopping. They return when they assume it's time for their number. If they happen to miss the appointment, they return the next day to try again. They have lots of time since many of them are on permanent disability or unemployment.[3]

When national health care was adopted for England, the National Health Service inherited a first class system with 350,000 staff members for 480,000 hospital beds. In 1991 there were 800,000 staff for 260,000 beds, and long "queue" lists waiting for hospital care (nearly one million patients waiting for hospital space).[4]

Anyone who believes that such inefficiencies are relegated only to the European socialized medical system needs to look no further than our own country. We have a totally socialized form of medicine that has been around for some 50 years: the Veterans Administration Hospitals.

The V.A. health care system now employs about 243,000 people, many thousands of whom earn in excess of $100,000 a year! In 1993 the V.A. budget was $16 billion. (By the way, all V.A. doctors and other health care providers are exempted from most personal liability for medical malpractice. There always seems to be a double standard when dealing with our government.)

I would suggest that, in addition to testing national health care on all federal employees, we include a mandatory reform of the V.A. system as a show of good faith.

Out of 26.7 million eligible veterans, less than 10 percent elect to utilize the totally *free* services of the V.A. Why? It's simple enough: service and quality.

The V.A. bureaucracy requires three volumes of the U.S. code (Title 38), a full volume of the code of federal regulations, plus several volumes of federal personnel regulations—all of which govern the moves of every V.A. employee.

Perhaps one of the patients at a Florida V.A. medical clinic described what eventually will become the standard at all medical clinics in America: "I pack a lunch and take a book. I go expecting to spend the entire day there. You eventually get to see a doctor."[5]

Not all V.A. facilities are poorly staffed and poorly run. Like anything else, there are dedicated people who choose to serve others in every walk of life. But it would certainly appear that government service brings out the worst in those who live on taxpayers' money.

I would suggest that, in addition to testing national health care on all federal employees (and politicians), we include a mandatory reform of the V.A. system as a show of good faith. I also suggest that we give this thing at least a 100-year test before it is implemented into the private health care system.

I question the feasibility of that in our computerized society but, even more, I question the ability of our government to keep its hands off such revealing data, especially when sorting out the "productive" from the "nonproductive" elements of society.

To specifically eliminate the ability to select alternative care, the proposed Clinton plan has built-in restraints on paying or using doctors outside the assigned system. Doctors who attempt to practice medicine the old way, making private arrangements with their patients, will face criminal charges, penalties, and fines of up to $10,000 per event. How's that for access to your own doctor?[6]

Even the socialized systems in England, Canada, and Europe do not restrict freedom of access the way this plan proposes. Doctors there are allowed to practice outside the system after they have met their required number of patients per week, although the exact procedure varies in each system.

PRIVACY INVASION

Privacy of medical records is another major concern when discussing any type of national health care system. Under the Clin-

255

ton proposal, a national medical bank would be established, into which all medical data would be funneled. There is obviously some merit to pooling medical data and information but, without total anonymity, open health care records could lead to some horrendous abuses.[7]

We are hearing assurances that all information would be kept strictly confidential. I question the feasibility of that in our computerized society but, even more, I question the ability of our government to keep its hands off such revealing data, especially when sorting out the "productive" from the "nonproductive" elements of society.

I distinctly recall reading, when Social Security cards were issued, the law required (and still does) that the assigned numbers could be used for nothing but Social Security accounting. Now that same government is proposing to use our Social Security numbers to keep track of our medical records. I don't know how you feel, but I would just as soon not have the government prowling through my medical files.

A paraphrased Proverb says, "It is a wise man who looks ahead, sees a problem, and tries to avoid it. A fool proceeds without caution and will pay a penalty."

I trust you will keep this in mind when writing and calling your representatives about the national Health Security Act.

In summary: It may be bad for your health, and it's certain to be bad for the health of our economy.

* * * * *

One last comment: I was asked by a newspaper reporter if it bothered me to be labeled an alarmist by some people.

"Well," I told her, "I don't believe I'm an alarmist any more than someone who calls the fire department when there's smoke coming out of a neighbor's home. It's possible the smoke doesn't mean there's a fire, but it's highly likely."

God wants us to be involved, but not fearful. As Proverbs 3:5-6 says, *"Trust in the Lord with all your heart, and do not lean on your own understanding. In all your ways acknowledge Him, and He will make your paths straight."*

If our government leaders would do this, our problems would quickly disappear.

NOTES

1. Dana Priest, "Health Plan 5-Year Cost Estimated at $700 Billion," *The Wall Street Journal*, 9/10/93; Sara Fritz, "Answers to Questions About Clinton's Latest Health Plan," *Athens [GA] Daily News*, 10/28/93; David S. Broder, "Health Plan Spending to Be Off-Budget," *Washington Post*, 12/2/93.

2. "The Reaper-9/1/93," *Cornerstone Report*, 11/93.

3. Elizabeth McCaughey, "Price Controls on Health Care," *The Wall Street Journal*, 11/22/93.

4. Max Gammon, "Among Britain's Ills, A Health Care Crisis," *The Wall Street Journal*, 12/8/93.

5. Robert E. Bauman, "The V.A.'s War on Health," *The Wall Street Journal*, 12/6/93.

6. Elizabeth McCaughey, "Price Controls on Health Care," *The Wall Street Journal*, 11/22/93.

7. John Merline, "The Dark Side of Health Reform," *Investor's Business Daily*, 11/16/93.

Appendix A

THE PROBLEM OF GOVERNMENT WASTE

1. The following is reprinted with permission of Macmillan Publishing Company from *Burning Money: The Waste of Your Tax Dollars*, by J. Peter Grace. Copyright ©1984 by The Foundation for the President's Private Sector Survey on Cost Control, Inc. Mr. Grace served as chairman of President Reagan's Private Sector Survey on Cost Control (the Grace Commission).

The Federal government is the world's largest: power producer, insurer, lender, borrower, hospital system operator, landowner, tenant, holder of grazing land, timber seller, grain owner, warehouse operator, ship owner, and truck fleet operator. The Federal government owns and operates 436,000 nonmilitary vehicles. It has over 17,000 computers, 332 accounting systems, and over 100 payroll systems.

However, while many of the functions performed by business and government are comparable, there is an important difference. Business has to perform those functions efficiently and profitably if it is to survive. That is the discipline of the marketplace and competition ensures that an individual company simply cannot afford to maintain a bloated payroll or mismanage its cash or pay more than it has to for the goods and services it purchases. . . .

American taxpayers, however, allow their government to escape the discipline of the marketplace. We have given government a free hand to mismanage our affairs. We have done this by voting for Congressmen and Senators who have no conception of the terrible consequences that deficit spending will bring.

Managing Money. The [U.S.] government handles some $6.8 billion in transactions a day . . . but despite these enormous sums the government is years behind the private sector in developing modern budgeting and accounting systems. Nor is it familiar with the common business techniques of cash, loan, and debt management. Each department uses its own accounting systems (there are 332 incompatible accounting systems), making accurate government-wide analysis impossible. The government has issued, backed, or sponsored $848 billion in loans outstanding, but lacks adequate controls and thus is highly vulnerable to substantial losses due to error or outright fraud. Government budgeting is mainly concerned with getting next year's spending levels approved, while, in the private sector, results versus what was budgeted in previous years are also examined. Compared to private business, Federal budgeting is done in a vacuum, where past budgets are forever forgotten, and there is little accountability. The Federal government has an annual cash flow of $1.7 trillion; however, cash-management procedures are so poor that money sits idle in non-interest-bearing accounts, costing taxpayers billions of dollars each year.

Will the Real Budget Please Stand Up? The Federal budget greatly understates the true level of Federal activity. First, the government practice of "offsetting" (deducting from spending) amounts collected from loan repayments and the like distorts the picture of actual spending levels. Then, the "off-budget" Federal

Financing Bank hides more government spending by offering the Federal agencies a "back door" to the Treasury. . . .

The Impact of Not Buying Prudently. In fiscal 1982, a typical year, the Federal government bought $159 billion in goods and services. Sixty billion dollars of that went for military weapons, the remainder for various goods and services across government. Some $41 billion worth of inventories were stored in hundreds of locations around the country. But the 130,000 Federal procurement personnel—government shoppers—find it difficult to recognize a bargain when they see one. First, they are entangled in over 80,000 pages of procurement regulations, plus 20,000 pages of revisions each year. Besides that, they work with inaccurate information, and their buying is often poorly planned and uncoordinated. You've read stories of the government paying $91 for a 3-cent hardware store screw. What is even more worrisome is that the big items—aircraft, turbines, rockets—are not bought with any greater concern for how much is paid out. The opportunity for fraud and abuse is immense. It is shameful but true that some government contractors get rich by hugely overcharging the government. . . .

The Cost of Not Watching the Store. The Federal government doesn't pay enough attention to the little things—housekeeping, travel, freight, mailing, printing, and so on; it doesn't even know how much many of these functions cost in total. They never tote this up and never look back. The result is excessive costs amounting to tens of billions of dollars a year. But there's no incentive to watch these activities. In fiscal 1982, the government spent $4.8 billion on employee travel. Because of the amount of travel, the government ought to have an in-house travel service, as most corporations do, to negotiate discounts and to efficiently book employee travel. But again, nobody in Washington cares about details. It isn't their money that they're wasting—it's yours. . . .

At the start of our commission's work, we were appalled at the Federal government's lack of basic information on its own activities. Some records aren't kept for more than a year, and others are not kept at all. Some figures are available for certain years but not others. . . .

When we started our work, we tried to find out how many social programs there are. "Oh, about one hundred and twenty-five," we were told. Then we found the book *Fat City*, which describes hundreds of Federal programs that give money away for nonessential purposes—at the expense of taxpayers. We went back to the drawing board and spent six months looking into the question of how many government social programs there are. We found that there are 963 social programs. Somebody in Washington should have known the correct answer—125 was only 13 percent of the true total. That's what we found out over and over again in Washington—somebody should know, but nobody does. . . .

2. Some recent examples of what your taxes are paying for (sources: Citizens Against Government Waste, the Heritage Foundation, and the National Taxpayers Union):

- $49 million for a rock-and-roll museum
- $15 million to Dartmouth College as part of a jobs-creation program—a total of thirty-nine jobs were created, at a cost of $324,685 each
- $1.36 million for preliminary work on an $18.6 million project to turn Miami Boulevard into an "exotic garden for people"
- $566 million (rising to $900 million later in 1991) to send American cows to Europe to participate in an "Export Enhancement Program"
- $500,000 to study the effects of cigarette smoking on dogs
- $107,000 to study the mating habits of Japanese quail
- $19 million to study whether belching by cows and other livestock harms the ozone
- $84,000 to study why people fall in love
- $50,000 to prove that sheepdogs do, in fact, protect sheep
- $46,000 to determine how long it takes to cook breakfast eggs
- $90,000 to study the social and behavioral aspects of vegetarianism

- $219,592 to teach college students how to watch television
- $2,500 to investigate the causes of rudeness, lying, and cheating on tennis courts
- $25,000 to find the best location for a new gym for the House of Representatives
- $2 million to renovate one of the House restaurants
- $350,000 to renovate the House beauty parlor
- $6 million to upgrade the Senate subway system

3. Organizations working to fight government waste and inefficiency:

Americans to Limit Congressional Terms
900 2nd St NE Ste 200
Washington DC 20002

> Donation includes a subscription to their newsletter

Citizens Against Government Waste
1301 Connecticut Ave NW Ste 400
Washington DC 20036

> Donation includes a subscription to the newsletter "Government Wastewatch."

Citizens for a Sound Economy
470 L'enfant Plz SW
East Bldg Ste 7112
Washington DC 20024

> Membership is $15 and includes a subscription to the newsletter "On Alert."

Freedom Alliance
PO Box 96700
Washington DC 20090

> Donation includes a subscription to the newsletter "The Free American."

National Taxpayers Union
325 Pennsylvania Ave SE
Washington DC 20003

Membership is $15, including a subscription to the newsletter "Dollars & Sense."

Appendix B

RESOURCE
MATERIAL

I. Articles and Excerpts
   A. Information provided by the Federal Reserve.
      1. Federal receipts, outlays, and debt, 1981-92.
      2. Government employment and finances, 1791-1970.
      3. Public debt of the federal government, 1791-1970.
      4. Federal budget summary 1945-1989.
   B. World Facts in Brief. Chicago: Rand McNally & Co., 1986.
   C. Administrative Office of the U.S. Courts Annual Reports, 1988.
   D. Health, a Concern for Every American. Wylie, TX: Information Plus, 1991.
      Energy, An Issue of the 90s. Wylie, TX: Information Plus, 1991.
   E. U.S. Bureau of Census, 1988, 1990.
   F. Facts on File World News Digest. NY: Facts on File, Dec. 1985, Dec. 1989, Dec. 1990.

G. Economic Indicators. Washington, D.C.: U.S. Government Printing Office, May 1991.

H. Robert Pollin. Deeper in Debt. Washington, D.C.: Economic Policy Institute, Nov. 1990.

I. A Survey of Current Business. U.S. Bureau of Economic Analysis, June 1989.

II. Book and Pamplet References

A. *War on Waste*. The President's Private Sector Survey on Cost Control. New York: Macmillan, 1984.

B. Harry E. Figgie, Jr. *Tackle the Debt Before It's Too Late*. Figgie International Public Affairs Department, 4420 Sherwin Rd, Willoughby, OH 44094.

C. Bruce Wetterau. *The New York Public Library Book of Chronologies*. New York: Prentice-Hall, 1990.

D. Ravi Batra. *The Great Depression of 1990*. New York: Simon & Schuster, 1987.

E. *The McGraw-Hill Dictionary of Modern Economics*. New York: McGraw-Hill, 1973.

F. Gerald Swanson. *The Hyperinflation Survival Guide*. Willoughby, OH: Figgie International, 1989.

G. James McKeever. *End Times Digest*. Omega Ministries, Box 0, Eagle Point, OR.

H. Arthur Zeikel. *History As a Guide*. Merrill Lynch Asset Management, 1991.

I. Ludwig Von Mises. "Money, Method, and the Marketplace" (essays). Norwell, MA: Kluwer Academic Publishers, 1990.

J. James Joy Ferris. *Inflation: The Ultimate Graven Image*. Harrison, AR: New Leaf, 1982.

K. James McKeever. *The AIDS Plague*. Medford, OR: Omega Publications, 1986.

Christian
Financial
Concepts

Teaching God's Principles of Handling Money

Larry Burkett, founder and president of Christian Financial Concepts, is the best-selling author of 18 books. The books are just a part of CFC's outreach. Larry also hosts two daily radio programs worldwide. The five-minute "How to Manage Your Money" is heard on over 1,100 outlets, and the live, thirty-minute call-in program, "Money Matters," is heard on over 475 outlets.

Larry holds degrees in marketing and finance, and for several years served as a manager in the space program at Cape Canaveral, Florida. He also has been vice president of an electronics manufacturing firm. Larry's education, business experience, and solid understanding of God's Word enable him to give practical, Bible-based financial counsel to families, churches, and businesses.

Founded in 1976, Christian Financial Concepts is a nonprofit, nondenominational ministry dedicated to helping God's people gain a clear understanding of how to manage their money according to scriptural principles. While practical assistance is provided on many levels, the purpose of CFC is simply *to bring glory to God by freeing His people from financial bondage so they may serve Him to their utmost.*

One major avenue of ministry involves the training of volunteers in budget and debt counseling and linking them with financially troubled families and individuals through a nationwide referral network. CFC also provides financial management seminars and workshops for churches and other groups. (Formats available include audio, video, video with moderator, and live instruction.) A full line of printed and audio-visual materials related to money management is available through CFC's materials department (1-800-722-1976).

Career Pathways, another outreach of Christian Financial Concepts, helps teenagers and adults find their occupational calling. The Career Pathways "Testing Package" gauges a person's work priorities, skills, vocational interests, and personality. Reports in each of these areas define a person's strengths, weaknesses, and unique, God-given pattern for work.

For further information about the ministry of Christian Financial Concepts, write to:

Christian Financial Concepts, Inc.
PO Box 2377
Gainesville, Georgia 30503-2377

Editing:
Adeline Griffith
Christian Financial Concepts
Gainesville, Georgia

Cover Design:
Joe Ragont Studios
Rolling Meadows, Illinois

Printing and Binding:
Arcata Graphics Martinsburg
Martinsburg, West Virginia

Cover Printing:
Phoenix Color Corporation
Long Island City, New York

Moody Press, a ministry of the Moody Bible Institute,
is designed for education, evangelization, and edification.
If we may assist you in knowing more about Christ
and the Christian life, please write us without obligation:
Moody Press, c/o MLM, Chicago, Illinois 60610.